George Farmer's

FARMER'S YEAR

A VERSE DRAMA FOR VOICES

LIST OF CHARACTERS

NARRATOR)	George Farmer, speaks clearly – in 70s, London accent
GEORGE FARMER)	speaks through windpipe wound, rasping sound
HANNAH SERVICE	aged 14, rural Co Antrim girl; teenage mother
DOG WALKER	tough-sounding man
IAN McNULTY	in his 70s, Co Antrim farmer, George's cousin
GORDON McNULTY	about 70, Co Antrim farmer, Ian's brother
WAYNE McNULTY	about 19, Gordon's son
CLINT McNULTY	aged 16, then 17, Gordon's son
ADAM BUTCHER	in his early 60s, the McNulty's neighbour, businessman
PRIMROSE CLABBY	in her late 60s, McNulty's neighbour, lady farmer
VIOLET CLABBY	in her 30s, Primrose's daughter
LARRY CULLEN	late middle-age, local small farmer, 'tramp'
ANDY COYLE	middle-aged, AI station manager
VET	Mary, in her 20s
HUNTSMAN	arrogant
JIMMY DOODY	middle-aged, local bailiff
LOCAL FARMER	at the market, associate of Ian's
JESS	George's collie dog
HUNT'S DOGS	
STAR	Hannah's horse
HUNT HORSES	

FARMER'S YEAR

A

39 C

First edition published in 2005

by Poetry Monthly Press

ISBN: 1-905126-36-0

Cover artwork: *Martin Holroyd*

Price:£5.00, €8.00 US$8.00

CONTENTS

PROEM

NARRATOR

Three score years and ten I've walked this earth,
To reach this time of contemplation, regret,
Satisfaction, intent on expressing, one last attempt,
All my gleaned fury, sorrow and mirth.

George Farmer – my name no longer in lights:
Faded into splotched celluloid my nights
Before live cameras in that TV drama
That gave me such a Sixties Wonderlad aura.

Belfast boy made good on the London stage,
Now home to Ulster in decrepit old age;
When they operated on my throat cancer
I refused the indignity of a voice synthesiser.

Virtually mute, I've skulked home to waste away
What time I've got left in the lush Six Mile Valley
I first discovered as a Wartime evacuee,
When Hitler's Blitz rained down on our wee city.

Farewell to North London's drive-by shootings,
Frequent burglaries, the constant thrash
Of capital life – I'll crash
In the countryside of my adolescent awakenings.

Here, I'll record for posterity the last ramblings
Of a jobbing actor who once commanded
Universal attention; the decades may have diminished
My profile and appearances but never wit nor feelings.

From amid rustic scenes wherein I dwell
I'll sing of what I love so well,
Though hollow winds and tumbling floods
And humming showers and moaning woods
All startle into sudden strife
And wake a mighty lay to life
Making amid their strains divine
All songs in vain so mean as mine.

JANUARY

[*Footsteps scrunch in frosty grass, ice cracks*.]

NARRATOR

It is New Year's Day morning. Scarlet twilight sears across the ridge of Tardree and Donegore, to unseen Knockagh where the war memorial pillar strains to touch the freshly risen sun. White wind turbines, angelic sentinels, cycle majestically on the horizon. A huge moon still stares mercilessly down upon the just and the unjust and up again, winking from the gently rippling surface of the noiseless, mirror-deep Six Mile River beside me.

Six Mile River: so named by the English soldiers in Plantation times, who rode from their camp to quench the thirst of their horses here; *Amhuin-na-fiodh* in Irish, this 'river of woods'. No forests now, all plundered long since; though this centuries old landlord's dyked sheugh I dander beside with Jess in our townland of Cullahill is sparsely lined with gnarled hawthorns and brittle ash. No forests now: that's why the Saxons first came, all those centuries ago: to denude this land of its timber, to consume in their hearths and smelting furnaces and to form the hulls of their trading vessels and war longships. An empire made good on stolen wood.

Jess bounds along the high banks of the ditch, while I shuffle through frost-hardened puddles and pristine-crystal glistening grass. The pale stalks of dead weeds and grasses stand tall above hardier rushes like the sprayed ornamental stuff that festoons vases in Christmas living rooms. Along the bank a heron rises, circles over the weir, soars skyward to descend beyond treetops. Jess's collar tinkles as she snuffles the scratched earth of a hole where, far within the warm-womb of soil, rabbit-life snuggles cosy and safe.

To our left, glides the river, a marshy field, then a high hedgerow before more hidden fields lead gradually to the incline where the hillsides rise to frame my pastoral idyll. To our right, beyond the sheugh and ministry, barbed- and netting-wire fences, a sheep-nibbled bare meadow humps to the clump of Victorian oak and sycamore that guard a lichen-studded, begrimed ring of boulders where once Druids chanted and performed blood sacrifices. Beyond that slumber Lylehill's prehistoric flint beds and the brightening, cloud-scattered sky.

From somewhere over there I hear the early gurgle-whine of a slurry agitator as Wayne prepares to empty tanks now the ground can stand the weight of tractors. Far enough away that the leeching toxins will filter through stones and soil before permeating through this land and along sheughs and streams to this trout-rich course; not far enough away.

Behind me, I leave the now deserted cottage, window-boarded, chimney-smokeless, roof-frozen, lifeless, that was once Billy Bell inhabited. They say towards the end, in his seventies, he'd take the bus to the city, worked as teaboy on building sites. One dark evening, he returned home to find his only companion, his bitch Milly, strung up from the lightbulb flex, lampshade askew, stiff as death; crude graffiti splattered blood-red on walls, drawers tipped out; the bad rips had even curled one down on top of the dining table.

Who's this? Up ahead, where the weir roars, creates a spray of frosty breath this winter morning. A young lass, leaning over the barbed wire fence, where a holly bush shines latex-like in burgeoning sunlight, berries red blazes of hope. She is offering a palmful of plucked grass to a sturdy, white mare, its sides straining with new life.

HANNAH
Hi, Mr Farmer! [*Jess barks.*] And hello to you, too, pup! Are you kissing me, eh? What's her name? Such a lovely wee dog!

GEORGE
Jess, behave! And who are you?

HANNAH
Hannah. Hannah Service.

GEORGE
Herbie's daughter? I was at school with him.

HANNAH
That'd be my Granda. My Daddy's called Herbie, too. He said you were back from London. Told me all about you. I've seen reruns on satellite TV of that *Copper's Lot* show you were in. And your throat – poor Mr Farmer. It's a shame you can't act anymore, can't speak properly. They say you're writing now. Poetry and scripts. Home to rural Antrim in your retirement. That's nice.

NARRATOR
Young Hannah – wavy auburn hair to her shoulders, face fresh as a spring pansy, cute in green Wellington boots, tight blue jeans, clumpy body-warmer over bright polo-neck jumper, cheeks and freckled nose flushed pink this winter morning. Thirty years younger, I'd likely swagger like Jagger, another pretty babe to tick off the list.

My heart aches for her beauty. But look at me: grey wisps of hair, flabby limbs and midriff, gaping hole at my Adam's apple, only covered by a flapping square of Band-Aid the same colour as the plastic tube that's sutured there, which I spue phlegm through as I whistle my stark words. And this girl is puzzling – there's evidence for her maturity, yet something seems wrong…

HANNAH
I nipped across the weir to check up on Star. Daddy's rented these fields for her.

I feel so sorry for her, bloated in her expectancy. For *obvious* reasons…

GEORGE
What age *are* you, Hannah?

HANNAH
Ah, I hear the disapproval in your tone! Like Daddy when Mummy told him for me. Me hiding behind the door, freezing in the hall – but shivering more out of fear than cold. Pregnant at my age – fourteen. How could it happen? They give us the facts in school, but – my mates talked how it was safe enough 'round that time of the month, you couldn't get caught. I though *they knew*… It was July, hay-time, a hot evening, he was walking me home from the bus after a Colin Farrell movie. We cuddled, like we would do, a wee snog…

GEORGE
That's how it begins!

HANNAH
Aye! Cuddling in the barn: balmy evening, moon and stars above. A sip of sweet cider, joking casually… It was so romantic, holding one another, touching, caressing, the urgency of love and longing… I don't regret it. A few moments of ecstasy in an otherwise barren existence. And I will care for my child so dearly, regardless of *his* present indifference. His callous entrapment.

GEORGE
His interest was… only physical?

HANNAH
(*Angrily*) Aye! I may be a fool, as Daddy says, to have gone along with him, but I'd a choice. And I chose love. And I can live with love, despite others'

heartlessness. But what do I need a boy for? A child I can rear, to share with me unconditional affection. Boys, I just don't understand those fickle creatures! They're too much bother. As Mummy says, I'm better aff wi'out a lazy, gormless, boozy eejit of a man.

GEORGE

Well, good luck to you, Hannah Service!

NARRATOR

Good luck to you indeed, as you withdraw your offered palm of grass from the horse's mouth, slouch back across the trickling weir to the wee cottages on the far bank, waddling towards swaddling clothes for your unplanned bundle of joy and tears.

Silly young fool; romantic dreamer; brave heart; good soul, *by treacherous love decoyed.* Too much too young. When I first lived here, at your age, Hannah, there was just as much foolishness or carelessness, call it what you will. But peoples' attitudes were much less forgiving or understanding then. Or was it? Tolerance? Well, blind eyes were turned, if it was spoken about at all, it was in disapproving whispers, women among themselves or a few men in huddles. Though those who faced such disgrace were generally less gracefully treated. There's something of human nature, at the basest level, in Hannah's predicament; the more things change, the more they stay the same. Ah, Hannah you've had your run in with your boy of summer in his ruin, laying the gold tithings barren, a boy of light who'd curdle in his folly, sour the boiling honey, a jack of fingering frost in the hives, full and foreign in the pouch. Like the lad I probably was, way back when.

The sheep in the meadow beside me as I amble on along the river bank with Jess towards my cousin's land, are home to early lambs bucking at the teat, tails wriggling atop upturned backsides. The flock starts to scent Jess's presence, swarms towards the far march hedge as we pass by. I stoop to leash Jess with a length of baler twine, continue on to the stile.

Who's this now? Huffing puffs of frosty breath he comes, lumbering towards me, cocooned in North Pole anorak, peaked hat complete with side flaps Velcroed beneath the chin, leather gloves, well-strapped hiking boots stomping through delicate crumbles of snow-crystals as high grass tumbles in his rough prints.

Two ugly, huge rotweilers, hideous as hell, all fangs and slobbering jowls, paws tearing up muck as they beeline for Jess. I haul Jess tight to my shin; she cowers behind my leg. One of these Cerberean brutes nuzzles to worry her, dunts against me. I raise my knee, give the heavy dog a shove away from myself and Jess.

DOG WALKER

(*Viciously, threateningly*) How dare you kick my dog! I'll put you in that river!

NARRATOR

I raise two fingers to my windpipe in order to rasp my reply all the louder, but the bullet-headed one moves forward, calling his dogs back. [*His shouts in background.*] Before you know it, his face is in my face.

DOG WALKER

Who do you think you are, kicking my pet, a dumb animal? You ought to be ashamed of yourself! I'll make you swim!

GEORGE

Don't you threaten me. *You're* trespassing.

DOG WALKER

Huh! He gives me lip! C'mon, oul' man, what are you waiting for?

GEORGE
You're the one issuing threats.

NARRATOR
He's squared up to me, but the longer he stands, the more we both know he's not going to throw the first punch. He backs away, with the brutes roaring at his heels.

DOG WALKER
C'mon Tyson, c'mon Bruno. *Your land*, huh!

NARRATOR
Off he goes, with a weak parting shot. As I gingerly climb the slippery wooden steps of the stile, cross our field he's just roamed through, my flushed cheeks begin to cool. I lead Jess past the dry cows chewing their cud – Ian must've been out recently, thrown them these liths of hay, gold-stalks stark on the frosty ground. I have to warn the likes of him off: what if the dogs had attacked the livestock, or he'd had an accident? Ian's insurance requires refusing permission, to avoid claims of negligence.

Jess picks up a plastic bottle in her mouth – flotsam from the river's last flood – and gambols ahead of me. I stomp wearily on, yet I revel also, though in my case it is inwardly, delighted by the picturesque twilight that has descended upon this snow-covered landscape of Cullahill, this 'back wood' of my retirement. Shortly, we meet Ian at the end of the back loanen, shooing calves into their shed in the yard.

IAN
Ah! Hi, George. These wee skitters bust a bar of the shed gate, hopped through it while I was tipping silage into the round feeder with the tractor grab. I'll hae te tie a pallet agin it fer now, till we get young Wayne t' weld it.

GEORGE
They've no water.

NARRATOR
I close Jess in the meal house, take some paling wire and poke it up the water trough pipejoint, which splutters. So it is with at least this little moment of satisfaction I leave the yard for my chilly caravan beside Ian's drab grey pebble-dashed farmhouse.

[*Sound of spurt of water and echoes of it filling the concrete trough.*]

FEBRUARY

[Sound of vehicle engine, then switched off; background car park and shop sounds.]

NARRATOR

A February nip's in the air sharp as a steel barb pricking the skin or a hard thorn spike embedding itself into flesh of finger or foot. I'm driving Ian's 4x4 to the chemists to pick up my prescription.

Passing the primary school, I see it's got a fancy new sign: their logo now is the castle gates. Soon, I pass that drystone archway itself, with its huge wooden green-painted, bolt-studded gates. Narrow slits remind me of ancient insecurity: this demesne was erected in Plantation times, when the English arrived to subdue the native Irish. Nowadays, older semis and terraces jostle with seventies estates and brand new courtyard apartments that attract yuppies to the expanding village.

There's oul' Tam's derelict end terrace house, along the main street of the old heart of the hamlet. He'd his carpenter's workshop out the back. I recall him heckling out of the side of his mouth. And I recall his tale of how, during the time of the land league disturbances, Tam's grandfather lay in wait for the landlord to pass by in his carriage, then let rip with a blunderbuss – the Right Honourable gent got the next boat to Liverpool, never came back, became a true absentee landlord.

The police station in this sleepy rural backwater is not like one of Northern Ireland's fortified barracks that the Troubles spawned: rather it is a square house of a building, rather like the traditional Garda barracks in any similar rural Irish settlement. The one difference is that this one squats behind a high wire security fence. A sign reads 'Closed'. A couple of police officers do come here for a few hours now and again to file paperwork or use the gym equipment, though only God knows when. If you need a cop in a hurry you phone Antrim, but the call gets rerouted to Toomebridge, some twenty miles away. I saw a couple of plods patrolling the other evening at nine; but still the car thieves enjoy their nocturnal forays unhindered. By the time you've phoned and the cops drive here, the hoods know they'll be long gone.

The main street used to have a few corner shops, but now Cullahill Post Office has moved into the filling station mini-mart; a Chinese takeaway, hairdressing salon, video nook, pharmacy and off licence congregate around its ever-packed car park. Only one old fellow sits on the bench outside, nursing a walking stick between his knees, slurping Red Bull till the offy opens.

But I have the pleasure of crossing the path of burly Adam Butcher, neighbour to my cousin, Gordon. Butcher's actually one of the old time locals, a riverside linen mill tenement urchin made good, now lording it in this rural retreat as a commuter-belt king. Adam's arm's in a sling. It's at times like this I'm glad of the throat, to be able to pretend I'm virtually mute.

ADAM
George! How's about ye? How's tricks?

GEORGE
Awright, Adam. You?

ADAM
Oh, the arm? Healing – itchy!. I suppose you heard I'd an accident thanks to that clumsy oaf of a neighbour of your's? It's really cost me a packet – I've not been able to attend to my business as much as usual. Well, *tempus fugit*. Must run. See you.

NARRATOR
Ah, I see, the wife's driving him. Too fat and lazy to walk to the shop. Wife – or is it his mistress? They say a couple of year's ago he was arrested at the airport,

stepping off a plane after a holiday to Marbella. It was a girlfriend on his arm, not the missis. Or a secretary, or some such. It *does actually* happen. The fraud squad were after Adam for 'financial irregularities'. He's a partner in a restaurant, as well as being an egg merchant.

I did hear about his broken arm: he tripped on some wire in his own field, behind his broiler houses, he says, claiming it was Gordon and his son's fault he had the accident. Gordon told Ian and me that Adam's insurance company chickened out, settled out of court. Thran Gordon went it alone. They were supposed to get the verdict this morning, which is likely why Adam's checking out how the *Belfast Telegraph* has covered the case. But Butcher's giving nothing away.

So, it's back to Ian's Hill Field, to get on with the ploughing I was doing. I drive past Primrose Clabby's place: round bales of silage have, painted on their black plastic wrapping, the legend:

Back off rural life - Stop the Rural Exodus.

Arriving in Ian's farmyard, there's the huge cattle lorry his nephews transport their motorbikes in. The young lads' names are emblazoned on the side in late-Seventies, *Fame!*-style script. They truck to the Isle of Man TT, the North-West 200 and other circuits to risk their necks, speeding on two thin tyres. Wayne's vying to be a computer technician; Clint wants to train as a pilot. Rural exodus: the young don't foresee a living let alone a future for them in shovelling dung.

[*Tractor engine sounds as George uses this vehicle now.*]

I mount my Massey Ferguson and trundle to the Hill Field. I've got two-thirds of the field ploughed already, head for the far side, a breeze beneath the roll bar cooling my ears. There's Primrose Clabby out on her Davy Brown, chugging up the same hill on the other side of the hedge that splits this slope. Her daughter

Violet's bouncing about in the link box on the three-point hydraulic linkage system at the back – that invention pioneered by Ulster's engineering genius, Harry Ferguson. A big burly woman dressed in duncher, Wellingtons and overalls like a drag Winston Churchill, Primrose waves cheerily at me and steers her tractor to the march hedge to yarn.

PRIMROSE
Man, what a day we've had, George! Went to the mart – depressing or what? Prices are back *again*. Those supermarkets and big processors are buyin' cheap meat from South America and we can't compete! And afore that Violet and I were in town, at the solicitors. Went to see if my other daughter Daisy's planning permission could be got. We're after a retirement bungalow. For me, *officially*; for Daisy, actually. Same odds. But they won't let us. You need to put a new build behind two hedges so it can't be seen from the road, and all our ground's too near the main line. Y' need to be in the Masons or something, I guess, to swing it nowadays. Or know a councillor, *very handy*, perhaps.

VIOLET
Yeah, Mum, know a councillor in the Biblical sense! Strange, too, have you noticed, how prostitutes always loiter in the streets round the town hall?

PRIMROSE
You may have noticed, George, my daughter hasn't much time fer politicians. It's not like the time Ian put up a tin shack in thont front field of his, the time he married. The bloody planners make it so hard for folk to build now, there's less folk *in* the countryside.

VIOLET
They've all had t' go to these estates on the outskirts of the towns, miles away. That means there's no one to use village shops, or schools, or post offices, and the

hamlets and villages are becoming either urban sprawls or ghost towns. *Rural living* is being destroyed by design!

PRIMROSE

Violet's a virulent campaigner when it comes to these suits interferrin'!

VIOLET

(*Chanting*) Have a care! Have a care! Support us
In our Campaign Against the Rural Exodus!

PRIMROSE

And I see, George, your other cousin, Gordon's secured a phyrric victory th' day.

GEORGE

Did he win against Adam Butcher?

PRIMROSE

We kinda 'overheard' the lawyers. The judge agreed the wire Adam tripped on wasn't Ian's, but he made both parties pay their own costs.

VIOLET

They reckon it'll cost Gordie about six grand in barrister costs, etcetera, etcetera.

GEORGE

Rough justice!

PRIMROSE

Pardon me t' hell fer sayin' so, but your Gordon's always been a thran oul' blert.

VIOLET
His back fields lie into Ian's, and they fell out once over Gordie openin' out a sheugh into Ian's drain. They went to law over that – imagine, and them brothers.

GEORGE
Ian maybe wouldn't let Gordon do it even if he'd asked nice. Another thran blert!

PRIMROSE
Course, their bad feelin' stems from Gordon bein' sent as a wean to oul' Rab McNabb's to help him wi' the milkin'. After ten years of servitude didn't Rab leave the place till Gordon. And there was Ian cartin' cattle in his oul' jalopy of a lorry from mart t' mart for a few shillin', wi' only a wheen-a scraggly bullocks t' his name.

GEORGE
His father left him the home place.

PRIMROSE
Aye, donkeys years on. Jealousy! Mind, both lads have ended up steady enough on their feet – when Ian was t' marry, y' know, he always took a power o' drink…

VIOLET
Ian McNulty? Never!

PRIMROSE
But the wife made him stap. Soon as he wed, he never touched another drap in anger.

VIOLET
You wonder how folk get by, rearing a family on what? Fresh air and sweat?

PRIMROSE
Aye, and them pair did it honest, too. Unlike Adam Butcher's oul' da.

GEORGE
Dan, Dan the funny wee man!

PRIMROSE
He used to sneak about the clumps of whin of a Sunday afternoon, tryin' to spy on the young 'uns like ourselves courtin' in the seclusion of the bushes, eh, George?

GEORGE
Dirty oul' Dan!

PRIMROSE
D' you remember, George, during the War, oul' Bill Scott reckoned he was losin' eggs, so wan time he sut in the chicken coop all night till his prey arrived. Wasn't it Dan Butcher – he got a shock when he deuked in the hen hoose door an' found himself starin' down double barrels! Billy let a rip jist to see him accelerate!

VIOLET
They must've been lean times, then, for folk that didn't have land of their own. Ironic, isn't it, how Adam's now an egg producer in a big way! While Ian and Gordon are strugglin', like most fermers.

PRIMROSE
Well, apart from that, I heard Gordon had a short fuse wi' Ian this mornin'. When Ian heard the result of the court case, he riled Gordon something rotten!

GEORGE
Oh dear.

PRIMROSE

Aye! I'd keep out of the big house th' night, if I was you, George, keep yourself to your trailer fer a quiet life! Gordon's bound t' be on at Ian, t' get his own back. There'll be some tonguin' goin' back an' forth fer a while yit. Well, you've yer ploughin' t' finish, George, we mustn't be keeping ya. (*Sighing*) Aye! I remember you as a young buck, George, ploughin' this hill on Christmas Day with a team of horses.

GEORGE

Yes, on Christmas Day, too! I walked rigs till I gave myself flat feet.

PRIMROSE

From the Hollywood Arches to fallen arches! That was wee Geordie Farmer, Violet – no but a strip of a lad out from Blitz-smoulderin' Bulfast for the duration.

GEORGE

I ploughed that day with Donald and Bathsheba, two horses that escaped the bombing of Wilton's funeral parlour, where me da worked – when they rebuilt it they got motor hearses, so the shires were sold off , and Ian and Gordon's da got first refusal.

PRIMROSE

Till ye acted in that Christmas play at the church hall, and stole the show, and headed for the Group Theatre in th' town. And then to London, the TV star, big-time actor.

VIOLET

And now you're back home, you've come full circle almost.

GEORGE
Like working in a field, passing round and round, or returning to the same cycle of husbandry season after season.

PRIMROSE
Like Ian and Gordon McNulty fallin' out, then fallin' in tillgether as mates awhile, then rowin' again!

[*Sound of their laughter; tractor engines rev up, fade into distance.*]

MARCH

[*Appropriate tractor engine sounds during the first three paragraphs below; appropriate cattle noises from paragraph six on.*]

NARRATOR

March comes in like a lion, with its roar of thunderous wind, fury of snow flurries, a late winter rampage across the river valley leaving beasts stranded beyond hedge-high drifts. The delicate purple, white and yellow flowers of the crocus bulbs I slipped into the soil around my frost-strewn caravan at the back end of last year are now flatten with the daffodils and first wild primroses beneath sheets of icy frigidity, their roots made rigid to cracking point by the solidified moisture in their beds.

Keeping active as ever, I let cousin Ian redd up at the home place, go to the outfarm at Shaneoguestown, a load of hay bales in a link box on the back on the big, red Massey 590 tractor. I rip along rutted roads at twenty miles an hour, and for once the drivers of the cars trailing me along the main road have relieved rather than impatient expressions on their faces.

Turning off onto the country road, I soon reach the railway bridge, nine feet clearance, which straddles a dip. It's filled deep with snow. Even this massive machine can't negotiate it; and I've no front bucket with which to dig a way through.

There's nothing for it but to abandon the tractor and lug two bales at a time along the powder-strewn path that is a yard higher than the road surface, through the bridge. The bales rhythmically bump off the tubular hand railings and my thighs as I step along. The weight of the bales pulls at elbow joints till they ache; the twine scrapes fingers and palms raw, through cold, damp, heavy woollen gloves. I've to set down my load from time to time, pause a moment as frosty breath billows from my nostrils, mouth and the loose Band Aid at my throat.

I have time, despite the agony and exertion of my task, to look up at the brightening sky framed by the dry stone archway, appreciate this morning's grandeur.

When I reach the field gate beyond the bridge path, I heave each bale over in turn, then climb after. I haul the bales up the brae. Reaching the crest of the land's slope, the lithe heifers see me from where they are nibbling at tufts of frosty grass at the far hedge, come galloping, divots of dirt flying from their hooves. I tug the two twine cords from round the first bale, scatter liths of dusty golden fodder to the delighted, baawing heifers.

I turn to see Clint, Gordon's younger son, tossing the rest of my bales over the gate to me. Grabbing two, I quickly release one from its twine. Clint's already hopped over the gate, opened the rest with a penknife, quick as jumping jack flash.

CLINT
Are ye stuck in the snow, George?

GEORGE
It's great to be young and fit, Clint! You're a great help.

CLINT
It's nay baather! Quare snow, eh? Da says we get a hooley like this every fifteen to twenty years. It was wild last night. Da sent me up to oul' Drew Pinkerton's to check up on him, as he's got a couple of sucklers in the house for calving. One was about to drap the calf, so I hung around. The blizzards across that wide yard of his are fierce.

GEORGE
Drew the Screw.

CLINT
I thought he was called that because he would try t' screw ye for any bob he could get in a deal.

GEORGE
So he does.

CLINT
Aye, but now I reckon there's more to it. The calf'd just been born, I was hunkered in the warm shed, I'd wiped the slime aff its face wi' strow, was watching it tottering on its scrawny legs, angling beneath the dam for a teet, when I realised oul' Drew's han' was on my thigh, felt his hot touch through the denim of me muck-spattered Levi's, was aware-a his oniony breath agin me neck.

GEORGE
Blimey! What did you do, Clint?

CLINT
I got the Hell outta that! Not my scene, y'understand. Diff'rent strokes fer diff'rent blokes an' aw' that, but he's a bachelor in his late Sixties an' I'm only sixteen. The calf was delivered, I'd done all I was gonna do fer him! I feared things might get outta han'. Or he'd try to take things *into* his own han's…

GEORGE
[*Guffawing*] I'm sure he's a harmless enough oul' critter. Just a lonely soul.

CLINT
Well, he caught *me* unawares! Jist tryin' his luck, I guess, misjudged the response.

GEORGE
Y'never know Clint, if he likes you, he might take you in – you'd get his place in a wheen-a years' time!

CLINT
Da says there's no point lickin' round oul' Drew, he's willin' his place t' the church.
Da an' Wayne are always doin' me down, chidin' me for bein' wee, weer than Wayne was at my age. It's the Stout filled him out: he started suppin' thon't black death at twelve or thirteen. Just because I'm less bullish in attitude when it comes t' dealin' wi' folk. Is it a fault to see both sides? Or be less trenchant in opinion? I can't wait till I'm up another few years an' out of it. This life. This country, too: *Norn Iron*, where everybody's the salt of the earth yet they're so quick t' come to blows over stuff I care little about and there's no easy fix to. Why can't they just let each ither alane and get on wi' their own lives? Peace process? Phoney recess..!

GEORGE
It's human nature, the world over – rumblin' in the jungle.

CLINT
[*Sighing*] Such is life. But I'm preparin' for the future: I've been takin' flying lessons at Newtownards. It's ace! Circling round Scrabo Tower in a two seater! An' the trainer says I'm a divvy at it – so fingers crossed I'll be a pilot afore long. Well, George, I have to head back to the yard, finish my chores. Will you get hame alright?

GEORGE

Sure.

CLINT

All the best then…

NARRATOR

And so we coped with the snow. And when the thaw came our idyllic little piece of rural Antrim was engulfed in floods as the Six Mile River swamped its banks. The drills in the fields sat too damp to get potato seed in for ages. Cattle in slatted yards were wading through slurry that seeped to overflowing, as their silage clamps ran short of bittersweet fodder and we had to cart black-wrapped bales from laneways.

It was as I was sloshing through lake-like puddles in cousin Ian's bottom yard one dark evening that I encountered Clint again. I was just heading across to the low, board-built pig unit, where Ian was injecting the latest batch of his weaners. I'd just got another bottle of iron solution and a fresh needle for the syringe from the box in his utility room, when a pair of headlights appeared through the driving rain. His brother Gordon's R-plated Animal pick-up trundled into the yard, splashing to a halt beside me. There were two plain but fresh-fleshed girls, all trussed up in polo-neck jumpers and anoraks, perched on the front bench beside Clint, who was driving. A gangly, ginger-bapped mate of Clint's was peering out from the back, where his cramped seat couldn't have been comfortable.

GEORGE

You've turned seventeen?

CLINT

Aye! And I passed the driving test three days after me birthday! Took it wearing me wellie boots! When you've driv tractors since the age of eight it's nay baather.

GEORGE
You're all dressed up.

CLINT
Half decent, I guess. Tell you what, George, we're doin' a Young Farmers' Club Treasure Hunt. I know, in this weather! Some stinkin' dark evenin', isn't it? But there you go. Y'see Uncle Ian's got some CARE posters somewhere. We've none.

GEORGE
Come on, then.

NARRATOR
I led him into the musty pig unit, not knowing quite how Ian would react.

[*Background grunting and snuffling of pigs.*]

CLINT
Ah, there you are, Uncle Ian.

IAN
Clint. To what do we owe this pleasure? Have ye come to aid us in our injectin' of these weaners? Aye, wee piggy, well may ye oink, you're about to get the prick of a needle in your hide.

[*Squeal of piglet as it is injected.*]

GEORGE
Clint's got a jeep-load of wemen with him.

IAN

Startin' young, eh? I reckon you've no interest in the sows, then? You've your hands full already. Off to a perty? Or, heck, in this day an' age it'll be a discotecque.

CLINT
What it is is, we need a Farmers' Union poster for our Treasure Hunt. I know you always have those 'Campaign Against Rural Exodus' wans.

IAN
Aye, surely. There's a wee bundle in the corner, there. Help yourself.

CLINT
That's terrific! Thanks. All we need now's a picture of Queen's University, of all things. We've scoured oul' *Belfast Telegraph*s to no avail. You'd think Wayne would hae one, but no.

GEORGE
In my caravan. On the wall, I got an Honorary Degree a few years ago. Got a framed picture of the redbrick college. The door's not locked.

CLINT
Really? That's fab, thanks! See youse later. Don't get too wet in this hooley!

[*Sound of door slamming shut in the gale. In time, noise of pick-up revving up outside and driving off.*]

IAN

Clint's a right fella. He helped you thont time of the snow, you said. More nur oul' Gordon ever would-a done fer me half-times!

GEORGE

Wayne seems okay too. It's a pity they'll be moving away in a few years' time. Wayne's already at college digs during the week, isn't he?

IAN

I suppose I shouldn't be too hard on them. It's not like I've any weans of me own to leave the place till. It's cheerin' t' have the spunk of the young livenin' up the place. It's been desperate quiet here since I lost Louise. It's been some company for me, George, your comin' back here t' Cullahill. I know I'm mustard t'get on wi' an' I'm sorry if y'hae te make do wi' that draughty oul' trailer y' brought over from England. Sure, move int' the house again, George, we can try an' keep outta each other's way if either of us is in a thran mood.

GEORGE

It's okay as it is. We each need our space.

IAN

Mmm, suppose, me to mutter over me crossword puzzles, you t' scrawl your poems in your notepad. An', of course, I would have t' listen t' you moanin' about the stink of my cookin' mate. An' I couldn't stick the sight of thont bledy throat of yourn, spuin' out phlegm - disgustin'! Why the heck doncha get wan o' them voice synthesisers?

Will these storms niver cease?! Will the land niver dry so we can get the spuds in, and see the crops grow? Look how many calves and lambs we've lost this year due to this rotten weather. It's costin' me a fortune in buyin' extra silage. Global warming, they say, climate change! I thought it was supposed to warm up, be dry, not damp!

GEORGE
Move to Fermanagh…

IAN
Fermanagh? Are you daft, George? It used to be for nine months of the year the lakes were in Fermanagh, and for three months of the year Fermanagh was in the lakes. Now, it's the other way round.

GEORGE
Exactly – you could diversify – grow rice in paddy fields!

IAN
(*Brutally*) Ack, man, your head's cut!

[*Sound of a piglet squealing; a loud 'thwock' and silence.*]

GEORGE

[*Shocked*] Ian! What!? *What* did you do *that* for?!

IAN
What's up with you, George? H'int you never seen a buddy get rid-a a runt? Quick dunt of the back of the head on the wee wall here, painless an' quick. Here, throw thont out on the midden fer me.

GEORGE
That piglet was alive!

IAN
Ack sure, how lang do these runts last?

GEORGE
It *might've* lived. You could've *tried.*

IAN

I've seen it all before. Waste of time. They usually die. It's not worth the effort. You an' your saft townee ideas.

GEORGE
Heartless beast! Dose your pigs yourself!

[*The door slams shut with a blast of gale as George storms out of the pig unit. Sound of gale raging.*]

APRIL

[*Sound of billhook cutting through hedge.*]

WAYNE
How's she cuttin', George?!

GEORGE
Oh, hello Wayne! Okay, except for the nettle stings on my knees.

WAYNE
Clint said he saw you out here. There's machines for cuttin' hedges now, y'know. But, I suppose this is an awkward place to reach with a tractor. And all the floodin' recently after the snow and all's left everywhere as boggy as Ballymoney.

GEORGE
When fields lie in puddles, the farmer's year is thrown into muddles.

WAYNE
Say, George, you're a poet an' you didn't know it! What a job we had getting' the ground ready for spuds. Are you billhookin' this bit of hedge to give oul' Uncle Ian a good neighbourly hand?

GEORGE
It's to give myself something to do.

WAYNE
Aye! Sittin' in that oul' caravan would be no craic. And there's nothing like a bit of fresh air and exercise. I see you've redd the sheugh with the drag, too. Grand!

GEORGE
You're all dressed up, Wayne! Got a date?

WAYNE
Oh aye, the suit. Naw, I was at Badger Bailey's funeral with me da. Well, the church service. Da got me to bring him on home. He can't stand draughty graveyards. Look… here… with these binoculars, George. If you point them up the hillside there, over the far side of the valley, you can see the cemetery. Aye! See, look - dark suited mourners cluster round the hearse like soldier ants around their queen; so the sorrowful procession of departure is acted out again. Aye, oul' Badger Bailey went quick. Hey, I can see the Silver Fox! Oul' Tommy Fox, with that grey mane of his. Is it true what they say, that he stole Badger Bailey's wife off him?

GEORGE
More the fool she!

WAYNE
I heard she left Badger Bailey for thon dodgy scut Fox. But he went bankrupt, was banned from tradin'. She lost money, dumped him, ended up as a carer in an oul' people's home, eking out a living; wouldn't ask Badger to take her back.

GEORGE
Too proud?

WAYNE
Wise enough to know he'd send her packing! And there's Badger's brother, Bill. They say Badger let Bill use this warehouse he owned for some business venture, up the Clonadrum Road, and the deal was after a year Bill would settle up for it. But Bill never paid. So Badger landed in, locked it up, put security guards on the property. And Bill tried to run them out with a shotgun! Of course, the law sided

with Badger. And the poor oul' security guards got mega compo for stress after bein' threatened with a firearm. Bill was lucky, he'd a decent brief, he only got six months.

GEORGE
Talk about the wild west!

WAYNE
Aye, George, some folk are right cowboys. Mmm! What's the lovely smell?

GEORGE
Mint.

WAYNE
Of course, I smell the aroma of wild mint amongst the weeds on the ditch there, in the shadow of the hedge. Your toil has tumbled up a rich fragrance that's refreshing, cleansing after the dense smart of fetid clay.

GEORGE
Like toothpaste! Or glacier mints!

WAYNE
(Laughs) Fox's mints! What makes a guy like that, like Tommy Fox, the sly fox, creep into other people's coops, steal away their chicks?

NARRATOR
When Wayne so romantically and poetically expressed the idealism of youth, the distaste for betrayal, the hurt and jealousy of a partnership shattered by intrusion, all I could do was shrug my shoulders and shake my head sadly. But my eyes were stinging, because a sudden rush of regret rippled through my system. It was as every incident of my lovelife were apparent in an instant; - and an

overwhelming sensation of regret overcame me, how my poor ex-wife suffered; - the riot of emotions I must have unleashed in *her* system, with my series of rash, psychedelic Sixties, ultimately selfish, infidelities.

Not that Clara stayed with me – we remained in constant touch, through Simon, and shared our pain. Not that she stayed (*Sighs*) and now she's gone, forever, after her series of treatments, as all the knots of worry and lesions of disappointment and polyps of anger at my disregard for the sanctity of our relationship severed her attachment to any hope of contentment in this earthly existence.

WAYNE
Hey, George – I think there's a sheep in trouble.

NARRATOR
Wayne had been scanning the fields with the binoculars. On the dry hill field's slopes he'd spied a ewe on her belly.

WAYNE
I think we'd better check it out now. Take a break from that billhookin', George. The thicket doesn't grow that fast; it's never as stubborn as you think it'll be, and it isn't that hard to hack through once you put a mind to it.

NARRATOR

So Wayne and I trudged and splished our way across the hoof-rutted, waterlogged field. We climbed the gate, bar tied tight with baler twine, and passed each curious sheep's face, mouths chewing cud nonchalantly, their wool-heavy frames tottering toe-to-toe as sucking lambs bucked with their brows at the dams' udders, tails wriggling in the air like epileptic tassels.

WAYNE
That's her, there. She's one of the late lambers.

GEORGE
Got a big bag.

WAYNE
Full of milk, she's lambing alright.

NARRATOR
When we reached her, we saw she had a lamb's head protruding. Wayne investigated.

WAYNE
Aw! No front legs!

NARRATOR
The sheep struggled to her feet and zigzagged for some yards, till young Wayne got an arm around her neck again. He eased her to the dew-sparkled grass, whereupon I took his place. Her panicked breaths warmed the back of my hand. I stroked her convex snout, her wide eyes relaxed, her chest heaved less. Wayne worked at the other end, slipped the tiny head back into its slimy cocoon, his bare arm writhed within the ewe in search of tiny hooves. Over the wool tufts of the sheep's belly I saw brown, speckled legs. Wayne tugged till sweat smeared his brow and blood streaked along his arm.

GEORGE
No joy?

WAYNE
I'll have another feel, I think I know what the hold-up is. (*Moans*) Ohh!

GEORGE
Bad?

WAYNE
I thought it was a second lamb, stuck in the channel. But now I find – this lamb's got a second head, twisted back at the neck. The lamb's long dead. We'll have to get it out, to save the mother. I need something to get this other head out of the way. What else can we do? She'll be dead by the time a vet would get here.

GEORGE
All I have's a penknife.

NARRATOR
I offered him the implement. Wayne was able to slice with the point at the extra neck. New tissue parted, with a tug he separated bone and brought it out. With an expert movement, legs, remaining head, bloody gap, body and all sluiced onto the sodden grass beside us. The ewe lay head down on my forearm, eyes dulled by discomfort and distance. There was an old plastic fertilizer sack blown into a nearby clump of yellow-flowering, sticky-scented whin; Wayne freed this from the gorse and dumped the dead calf and amputated head into the bag and carried it back across the uneven meadow towards the yard. It was then that I noticed another unfortunate creature.

GEORGE
Only three legs!

WAYNE
Have you not noticed that ewe of Ian's before? There's a similar story – one morning I came across her on her back, the time Ian was poorly. A fox had eaten

the head off the lamb as it was only just emerging from the womb, and tore off the ewe's back leg.

GEORGE
'*Nature red in tooth and claw'*.

WAYNE
Indeed. So I tugged the remains of the dead lamb from her. I jagged her with penicillin, thinking there wasn't much hope for her, and fed her with a bottle of milk. The next two days, I did the same. She'd eaten a patch of grass around herself, so on the third morning I tossed her a lith of hay. The fourth day, she was gone; gone to the far corner of the field tottering on three legs, grazing away. With no lamb to suck, she's thriving as well as any of the rest of the flock, now.

GEORGE
And the wound wasn't sewn up?

WAYNE
When she got on her feet, it was too late, and besides I couldn't catch her to patch her up! So, I'll give our other unlucky lady here a jab of penicillin too, hope the trauma of the lost lamb doesn't affect her, or rather *in*fect her, dispense her with April's ultimate cruelty. (*Sighs*) There must be a better way than this, George.

NARRATOR
Wayne clearly disliked the blood and guts aspect of farming. The armour of Wayne's shell hadn't yet hardened to the same strength of resilience of that of his father, Gordon, or uncle, Ian. I knew where he was coming from. For all its pleasures, country living held other unpleasantnesses, as I discovered.

'*April is the cruellest month*': there I was being hounded by the black dog, as Winston Churchill called depression, and the deaths of innocent life, the suffering around me, made me feel low again. But I fought it, I wielded the stick of forbearance. And my billhook, to slash away again at the hedge.

Wayne muttered, 'There must be a better way than this' – of course, I know there is. But I didn't open my mouth. Too scared to look a fool, knowing how far reality is, and current attitudes are, from the ideal I aspire to for my land and my community. But simply knowing there is a better way, and resolving to speak up next time I have the chance, lifts my spirit. That and seeing the neat job my bushwhacking was making – a smile of satisfaction burgeoned across my face like the lengthening of spring evenings.

MAY

NARRATOR

The queen of months arrives with the hum
Of bees weighing down the flowerheads they feed upon,
Nosing pollen with all the bliss of seasoned junkies,
And with the thrum of silage machinery gliding
Symmetrically along swards, green mists of fine-chopped grass
Spuing from the harvester's spout into trailers.
I am stooped before a wrought-iron field gate,
Its metal thick and heavy as horseshoes,
Its pockmarked struts caked with decades
Of the same black bitumen paint I now slap
Onto it as silage trailers, hauled behind huge
Massey Fergusons and Fords rev by, dried crap
Flying from their tyres like golfer's divots.
The gate is hung between two round constructions
Which I've already whitewashed: true Ulster pillars.
A Ute stops beside me – it's Ian's brother, Gordon.

[*An Animal pick-up utility truck drives up beside George; the engine is switched off.*]

GORDON
Quare weather, George!

GEORGE
At last.

GORDON
Doin' a few repairs, eh? I saw the tops were off those pillars. What happened?

GEORGE
Vandals!

GORDON
What? Bad yins hae knocked down the capstones? In this day and age, there's nothing sacred. You're red-faced, and I'm not surprised you're in a rage, George. Who knocked them down? I can imagine: a couple of boyos staggerin' home a-night from the Ballygofey Arms. Stopped for a leak and decided it'ud be a geg t' topple the capstones. Wan each! And who was strangest? Who'd be first t' git his till th' ground? Doesn't it make y' sick?! Have they no respect for other people's property?! Look at the bother it's givin' ye, George!

GEORGE
I had to lift them up with the tractor front grab…

GORDON
Them things are a ton weight each. Easy four foot across, more, an' inches thick at the edge, more in the centre where they rise to its wee point. Ah! I see you've cemented them on, good on ye, George! That'll stop the boyos next time! But blimey, George, them things have sat there for hundreds of years. Y'know, a wheen o' years ago, Ian showed me this document the solicitor sent him. Now they've the land registry, the oul' deeds were cancelled, so they sent them to him, to save storage space, I guess. It was only first written up about 1903, at the time of the Land Acts. But it showed the owner from 1617 till then was an English Lord and his heirs. They got given it at the time of Plantation, by Royal Decree. Ian's place here was only sold to our grandfather, who was the existing tenant, in the 1920s. Wrought all his life to afford to buy the place. Our da, too, sweated t'

pay off the Land Annuities, the annual mortgage-like payments. It wasn't till '72 Ian and Da finished payin'. Some still are.

GEORGE
It's taken that long? Bloodsuckers!

GORDON
Ironic, isn't it, George, that the Catholics in this country always go on about having been 'dispossessed', but us ordinary Prods never got much out of 'our country' till recently. Our planter forebears suffered as much as any other buddy's.

GEORGE
Life's always a struggle.

GORDON
Aye. (*Bitterly*) But in Denmark, an' Scandinavia and them places, when the landlords freed their serfs in the nineteenth century, they treated them with more respect, more fairly. Grandda used to tell how his grandfather survived the Famine, as a wee boy, pickin' the tiny spuds from the fields, too small and hard to suffer blight, and kept them for the next year's seed. Man dear, when we're harvestin' a field of spuds th' day, those wee bucks git overlooked – not worth batherin' wi'.

GEORGE
Changed times.

GORDON
Mind you, I'll tell ye, George Farmer, for all the harm the landlords done, they drained the land and redd it up, planted the hedges and brought in good things,

too, like flax, that gave us our world famous linen trade. And built these sturdy Ulster pillars (*He slaps the wall with a hand*); it's such a shame, a couple of eejits would vandalise them. For good or bad, they're our history and our heritage.

GEORGE
A work of art's a work of art, no matter how odd or corrupt or disagreeable the artist.

GORDON
The big Lord upstairs, He works in mysterious ways, His wonders to perform. There'll be a curse on those rascals that did these pillars of Ulster harm!

GEORGE
(*Laughing heartily*) Hundreds of years, these here?

GORDON
Aye. And upturned in seconds by ignoramuses. Mind you, when you think about it, 1617 – the beginning of recorded history. *Their* history. As planters. As if what existed before that Year Zero didn't exist. It was when they *took, took* possession. And anything, everything, everyone before then was truly dispossessed. Not that I'm some surt-a rebel – I'm a true blue Orangeman, y' know, George. After all, some of them Irish lords before the English came in were right rogues, too. Sure, didn't their high kings visit the lesser kings, and when they came t' stay, they got the right t' sleep wi' the lesser kings' wives. Some houseguests thon! I'm just passin' remark, George, on the ironies of history and all that.

GEORGE
I know!

GORDON
Not that there's many o' us country Orangemen left. The young bucks dinnae want t' be bothered wi' it. Can y' blame them when y' see the surt-a rips they let int' the bands now? All the half of them crowd want is t' get full and get a fight started. And these well-heeled yuppies movin' in t' the area are far too busy playin' golf or summat. My own young uns, Wayne and Clint, they went to the band when they were young, but they've their discos and all and couldn't be bothered wi' the yahoos thonder, now. And they dinnae want t' farm either. Who can blame them fer that? Who wants t' farm when you dunno what you'll be getting'? When I was young, the Government had their five year plans, you knew ahead what t'expect, a buddy could be organised. Nowadays, it's potluck. And it's not enough…

GEORGE
Wayne and Clint seem to be good helpers.

GORDON
Ack! In our day, you were told what t' do by the oul' fella and you done it, and that was it. Nowadays, well… I wouldn't even ask them. They do a bit when it suits them. Sure, young 'uns would rather be out rakin' in kyars, or racin' them bikes, or playin' Halo on the X-Box than muckin' out a horsebox or reddin' up the yard.

[*A tractor and silage trailer rev past.*]

GEORGE
Another load of silage.

GORDON
A quare crop, it has to be said, despite this spring's unusual snows and floods.

It's glorious now it's May, with the swallows tweetering in the trees and starlings hopping from hedge to hedge. At last the tulips are resplendent in their multicolours, the bluebells carpet copses indigo as still as pacific oceans.

GEORGE
Makes you feel good to be alive.

GORDON
(*Awkward*) Aye, it does, George. Well, I've promises to keep and miles to go afore I sleep… Y'see thont pillars, why, I'd like t' lie in wait of a night with the shotgun, see what craythurs come by drunk, gabbin' of when they toppled the capstones, and I'd let rip a blast t'scare th' boyos!

GEORGE
You can't do that!

GORDON
No! Not nowadays! And that's progress! When the burglars can bust into somebody's home, like oul' Johnny Rodgers, and bate his face till it's purple, red an' blue as a pig's backside jagged wi' an iron shot, all for the sake of a fiver! And the court jist says, 'Ack, sure, it was a first offence' an' gie them a tickin' aff an' there's oul' Johnny found under the sofa wi' a heart attack an' nearly died. There's no justice in that! A buddy can't go aff t' do the chores but fear when he gets back some gypsies 'll have redd out the garage of the ride-on mower, socket set, hammers, wrenches, every damn tool it's taken a lifetime t' gather up. Wan day the swines took me mother's bootscraper from the backdoor step! And it was *her* mother's; it broke her heart.

GEORGE
It's a material world…

GORDON
Aye, George, they're only material things, but it's the sentimental value, eh? And that's a spiritual thing. And it's the principle of the situation – stealin's wrang!!

GEORGE
'The world is too much with us…'

GORDON
Well, I dunno about that, George, but I do know the thievin' hoors that take our stuff are too often wi' us! But I'm glad to see somebody who cares about things. Keep up the good work, George, paintin' and preservin' those gates. Nothin's sacred anymore.
Did I tell ye about the church? The committee at Ballygofey Presbyterian's only just plannin' t' knock down the church! It was built in the 1840s… I know it's not St Paul's nur anything, but our family and community history's tied up in that place. The pine sheeted ceiling's over a hundred years old. I reckon the pews are original, and the windows are sound.

GEORGE
A puritan shell. And the pews are hard as hell! Cut your bum to ribbons.

GORDON
But we were married there, family funerals and baptisms were held there… They want to raze to the ground that building in which we shared those solemn rites with our forbears. They reckon it'll cost at least half a million… Each family would have t' cough up an extra grand or two a year fer a decade in their freewill offering t' pay off the loan they'll need t' do the job.

GEORGE

I'm more individual in my faith, my approach to the Transcendental.

GORDON

Oh aye? Wan o' these Buddhists probably, knowin' you as wan of these trendy actors and London Bohemians.

GEORGE

Not Buddhist, no. Buddhism is impersonal – it doesn't account for any *individual* identity. But we are, each of us, unique souls, and God is…

GORDON

The Supersoul? Hah! I pick these things up, y' know! I'm not exactly stupid, now. An' we're made in His image – His spiritual image? There's a thought. I niver reckoned you to be a deep thinker, George. I thought you were more interested in a bit o' skirt than a bit o' vestment… Like it said in the papers, the Swingin' Sixties perty animal that could dhrink George Best under th' table an' bag more girls than Austin Powers. Maybe there's hope fer us all if you can repent.

GEORGE

There's hope for us all!

GORDON

Well, let's hope and pray we git this silage in afore thont dark clouds on the horizon tip down on us! By-jimminy, George, you don't half keep a buddy back from his work wi' your gabbin' and talkin' fool nonsense about politics an' religion and what-not. I'm away off afore really upset the kyart and start on about sex.

NARRATOR

The ebullient, straight-talking, ever-dissenting honest Ulsterman, Gordon McNulty. Sound as a pound in anyone's currency. I was feeling downcast that there are people in the world who do daft, thoughless things, like topple capstones off white Ulster pillars. But the mere fact that there are hearts and minds like Gordon's, for all his limitations, or petty local prejudices, or occasional thranness, is enough to restore my faith in human nature and natural wisdom.

[*Sound of pick-up truck driving off.]*

JUNE

[*Background sounds of people's voices, cattle bellowing.*]

NARRATOR

"Now summer is in flower and nature's hum
Is never silent round her sultry bloom
Insects as small as dust are never done
Wi' glittering dance and reeling in the sun..."

wrote John Clare of June. Similarly, today the cacophony of busyness about the farmyard is almost unbearable for a fragile oul' fella like me.

It's testing time. Although they don't get on whiles, Gordon has come to give his brother Ian 'a hand'. 'Neighbouring', it's still called; deriving no doubt from the *meithel*, or reaping parties in ancient lore, when scores of feudal peasants would scour the land for the golden grain. Extended family, or 'freens' as they're called today, in Ulster-Scots colloquial, and neighbours would come to each plot in turn, gather in the harvest in an act of communal sharing. An age-old custom curtailed by contemporary individualism, and the advent of mechanisation.

But it's testing time, not harvest time today in Cullahill. The suckler cows have to be brought in from the fields for tuberculosis and brucellosis testing by department of agriculture vets. Bovine TB has rendered several thousand farms in Northern Ireland quarantined. Lorryloads of cattle are driven off for slaughter when they fail these tests, their flesh often condemned as unfit for human consumption; a cull to prevent the spread of disease. Diseases that appear to be on the increase as their microscopic spores become resistant to antibiotics.

So Gordon and his sons have come to my cousin Ian McNulty's to help with the testing. The lean-to silo house is full of baawing cows, calves at their flanks. Gordon's boys will take this opportunity of bringing in the herd to castrate the bull calves and dehorn them all for Ian. Having given each head a local anasthetic injection, Wayne will use a gas-heated iron to gorge out the horn buds from the skull of each calf. Quick and no more painful than pulling a tooth, Ian says.

They've brought Larry Cullen with them, a local hobo. Straggly, colourless beard like a whitewashed whinbush, threadbare greatcoat tied round the waist with blue plastic baler twine, the entire yokel outfit bar the length of straw drooping from his mouth – instead, a cigarette is clenched between askew yellow, black and beige tobacco-stained pegs.

LARRY
Uck, man, if it isn't the Hollywood star himself! What about ye, George?

GEORGE
Holywood County Down, you mean?

LARRY
That's the big time round here! Snobtown!

NARRATOR
Larry slobbers his sentences through a grubby-cheeked grin. He carries a length of stick plucked from the hedge like some bedraggled wizard with makeshift wand in manure-splattered green Wellington boots. Ian, Gordon and the boys usher cows along the crush chute – a gap between the lean-to wall and this smaller wall – so the vet can nip a fold of their hide with his chrome measuring calipers as if giving a row of schoolchildren inoculations. Meanwhile, I endure Larry's attention.

LARRY
Did y' hear, George, the sister Elsie's deed an' gone this twelvemonth!

GEORGE
Sorry to hear that.

LARRY
Aye. She got whit ye hae, throat cancer. But she caught on what it was too late, and it was on through her insides afore the doctors cud do owt. At least you've managed to lick it, eh, George? I seen you at the clippin' wi' wee Wayne and Clint.

CLINT
Aye, Larry, George judged the Grand Sheep Clipping Contest for us!

WAYNE
Get over it, Clint – are ye still sick to the stomach that I bate ye?

NARRATOR
It was great to hear the young brothers' banter about our day in late May when they came to clip Ian's ewes. It reminded me of assisting when their father and my father clipped, when I was a wee fella. In this same yard. The constant clicking of shears and the sweaty aroma of wool…

LARRY
You're both wheekers at clippin', lads. Gie up there!

NARRATOR
Larry prods a cow's hip as it trots gingerly over slats towards the crush. The last lot have been released by Clint through the little gate at the far end of the crush. Wayne throws himself over the wall to help Larry and me round up the cows in the empty silo's cathedral-like, high-domed interior. Sunshine on the corrugated zinc roof has made this shed stifling on a breezeless afternoon.

WAYNE
I'll get that stray Hereford, Larry. George, you keep them other calves from getting by thonder, till we get her back round to Clint.

NARRATOR
From where I stand I can see into the shadowy lean-to. The wee calf skids, skittering along the concrete floor towards the far end. Wayne gets behind the cow. It's the big roany half-Hereford with horns that Ian got from Davy Exley at Ballymoney mart last autumn.

She's panicked that Wayne has separated her from her offspring, with a sudden lurch lowers her head. The buffet makes Wayne slip on fresh piss and shit on the smooth floor. He falls to the ground. The cow swipes at him with a sideways movement, one horn pins him against the side wall.

Wayne makes no sound. But his face is suddenly pale. Even from this distance I see the look of horror on his face.

The cow trots nonchalantly now, only a brief huff through its nostrils gives away its irritation as she leaves the lean-to with her calf at her side, passes Larry and me.

GORDON
(*Annoyed*) What are ye-es doin'? She's away now!

LARRY
(*Shouts*) Quit yer guldernin', Gordie, yer boy's hurted. She's gutted Wayne!

NARRATOR
Clint rushes forward, sees his brother sitting up against the wall of the cattle house, clutching his belly like an injured soldier against a tree in hostile territory. Clint fumbles for his mobile phone, to call for an ambulance. I reach young

Wayne, strip off my grimy white shirt to my sweaty vest, wrap the cotton across his stomach to staunch the flow of blood. Wayne is already too weak to put pressure on it himself, so I press the shirt against the ugly stain that seeps red-hot plasma. The blood trickles between my fingers, tickles the backs of my hands. So much blood.

GORDON
(*Concerned)* Put him in the jeep – we've no time to wait for an ambulance.

NARRATOR
So we lifted Wayne as carefully as we could, our arms shaking with shock and emotional agony as much as his own form trembled with pain. Larry drove. Not very fast, but in hindsight that was sensible. The ministry vet came with us, tried to help poor Wayne as best he could. At the hospital they rushed Wayne into Emergency and gave him a transfusion. The cow's horn had pierced deep. As the surgeons attempted to repair his damaged innards, I waited with Ian and Gordon. Ian was cussing himself, because it was his cow. Gordon just wanted silence, and good news. He sent Clint and me back to redd up at Ian's. A few of the cattle were still standing about in the yard.

IAN
Be careful of that roany, watch her…

NARRATOR
Ian advised us as we left. As the stunned Clint worked with me I tried not to think about the last time I'd been in this situation. Tried not to relive the bad dream of the evening when I was called to the north London hospital waiting room, the night my Simon was stabbed in a street brawl. *Brawl* the Old Bill called it – attack, more like! Saturday night, you know the scene, young lads out for a pub-crawl. Someone bumps against someone, or looks at them wrong, tempers and

tragedy.

This time, with Wayne, the doctors sent Gordon and his wife away, said Wayne was stable, though he was still in intensive care. My Simon only lasted a few hours, that's why I knew Wayne was going to be alright once he'd survived beyond that length of time.

The second night after it happened was when the monitors went mental, shrieked like barn cats.

The minister called with Gordon and his wife. Ian's only support was Larry Cullen and dumbstruck, uselessly silent me.

The morning after the incredible news, I did the chores for Ian, then took myself off across the fields, bleary-eyed from lack of sleep, with Jess. Jess scampering about as if nothing had changed. At the march hedge I heard Primrose Clabby's tractor ripping towards me.

PRIMROSE
George Farmer! Tell me it isn't true?! Gordon's boy's in the hospital? I saw Larry Cullen at the shap yesterday evenin' when I was getting' the *Belfast Telegraph.* Larry said they've gie him twenty-four pints of blood so far. I niver heard the like of it!

GEORGE
But he's gone, Primrose. Last night.

PRIMROSE
Oh George, I'm so sorry! All those transfusions and they couldn't save him? You know, I remember when you and I were young, George. My father and I came to McNulty's to help with shifting Ian's Da's herd – they'd broken through the march hedge and got intil our meadow. So, we walked them back round by the road. And youse had Sunday afternoon visitors – some relatives. They'd a

younster, a wee girl in a pretty blue dress, about three year old. There was a pile of rough sand in the yard and she'd been futtering about in it, playing at making a sandcastle I think. As one of the cows we were moving came trotting down the lane ahead of the rest, their collie affrighted the cow, an' she tuk aff down the yard, tail high. Headin' at a mighty gallop straight where the wee girl was sittin'. I was sure she was goin' t' trample over the wean. We all were – I could see the mother on the front doorstep, beside Mrs McNulty, hands raised to her mouth. But that cow, she saw the wee girl and with a spring like Jesse Owen, deft as a Grand National champion clearing Beechers Brook, she leapt over the wee girl – front hooves and back. Cantered on down the yard and back loanen without droppin' a single mph. Ah, George! Cows are usually considerate creatures! It's such a shame, fer poor Wayne – she must've thought her calf was in dire danger. The maternal desire to protect takes over, eh? She can't have *meant* harm – it was pure animal instinct, such as all creatures are prey to. *George!*

NARRATOR

I wept for my own loss as well as my family's. I cried over the seeming futility of flames that flickered into life in shades of obscurity which, nonetheless succeeded in their struggle to shine bright auras into the lives of those around them, only to be overwhelmed so soon by the surrounding darkness.

Primrose Clabby leaned over the barbed wire fence and wrapped her arms around my shoulders. That's when I discovered I was sobbing like a heartbroken girl. Through my tears I noticed young Violet skulking by their link box, embarrassed by my grief. Only that glimpse of future hope retained my sanity, renewed my strength.

PRIMROSE

(*With a cackle*) That's the first time in a long time I've got me arms round you, George Farmer! Indeed so, Violet, yer mother was once out on a date wi' this chappie! Imagine, me out wi' a star o' stage and screen!

GEORGE
It didn't work out, Violet. *She* was interested in Victor Clabby.

PRIMROSE
Could ye blame me? My Victor has a farm-a land comin' till him, you were jist a wee evacuee fram the big smoke, a backstreet urchin wi'out a bob till yer name.

GEORGE
Nothing's changed there!

PRIMROSE
Oh, I think you've made good for yourself.

GEORGE
Appearances can be deceiving – just because you're famous, that means nothing.

PRIMROSE
Well, that's true. Still an' all, we're not in the predicament of so many the world over, starvin' or sufferin' drought an' whatnot. Well, George, have I rekindled any spark of romantic interest wi' that cuddle?!

[*They all laugh heartily.*]

NARRATOR
I couldn't help but join Primrose and her daughter Violet in their laughter at my shocked silence. And so it was as I trod my weary way back to the yard, looking at the passive river below me, I smelt the ripeness of barley meadows again, felt the rising sun warm my face and arms, smiled as Jess skipped from rabbit hole to bush here and there, felt the exhaustion drain from my body.

JULY

[*Sounds of band music and vehicles to coincide with narrative/first few paragraphs.*]

NARRATOR

We pass the mound where a Norman fort stood, this motte high up in the valley that surveys several counties. Above this hill the sky's face is as morning fresh as a milkmaid's. My faithful collie Jess pauses to pick with her teeth at a sucking tick on her back, then squats, cocking a leg that trembles with effort and relief.

It's a bank holiday, but the garden centre is closed. No cashing in when the populace are off work today - it's the Twelfth of July and this is loyal Cullahill.

Through sultry summer haze I can see far below the roundabout where three coaches stand. There, new bunting and flags flicker in the breeze as the gathered bandsmen begin: the thump-thumping of lambeg drums resonates, someone tickles a martial tune from a flute. But their codding about ends abruptly as they board their buses and are soon gone: farmers, local businessmen, labourers, tradesmen, off for their annual parade beneath a sweltering July sun.

For all their pomp and self-importance their numbers have dwindled: the rural Orange hall better serves village fetes and jumble sales these days. I wonder to myself is Gordon there this year, does he have the heart for it so soon after his eldest son's death; has Clint turned out, to be with his father as they step out to show their community a brave face despite adversity and loss. Probably. More poignancy this year in their neighbour Patsy McFadden doing the chores about the yard for Gordon and family, in the light of Wayne's death. McFaddens being Catholics: the traditional 'neighbouring' extending in some parts still to the one side covering for the other on their parade day, reciprocated by Gordon's doing the same for Patsy come Hibernians' day, in August. A custom that, to my surprise, three decades of internecine violence hasn't eradicated; not in this backwater of Cullahill, at any rate.

Peace returns to Cullahill and Ballygofey as the coaches head for the dual carriageway. Until a distant helicopter buzzes forward, circles by, rotors whipping as it descends towards the RAF camp. I walk my long march with Jess to the footbridge over the motorway.

Vehicles swish beneath us. But there are less than usual. A young woman with a pushchair is spiralling up the walk ramp, approaching from the other end of this blue-railed, functional Nineteen-Seventies construction. With a sudden start of recognition I greet her, blurt...

GEORGE
Hannah Service?!

HANNAH
Uck, hello Mr Farmer! How's about ye th'day? Would y' look at the eyes nearly poppin' out of your head! Aye, this is my wee Will.

GEORGE

After Prince William?

HANNAH
No, silly – I named him after Will Young! Wee Will's three months now. It seems like I've had him forever. You get so used to a way of life so quickly, eh?

GEORGE
You'll have him all your life, now.

HANNAH
Aye! Well, till he's eighteen. Then he can get a place of his own!

GEORGE
You'll still be young then.

HANNAH
You tryin' t' rag me, George Farmer? I can handle it; I've got enough of it already. But I'm goin' back t' school in September, regardless of however much they look down their noses at me, or sneer at me, or tease me. Aye, when Will's eighteen I'll be… thirty-two? Naw! Sure, that's oul'!

GEORGE
(*Laughing*) No way! Are you not away to the Twelfth, Hannah?

HANNAH
No. Daddy and our Terry are away aff to it, but Mummy's in the house full of the 'flu, snatterin' away, so I'm stayin' wi' her. And Will, of course.

GEORGE
Is it difficult for you – to live at home?

HANNAH
It can be. My brothers are scunnered with the ba's gurnin'. I can't wait till I'm old enough to put in for a place of me own. My cousin Irene's got her own flat in the town.

GEORGE
(*Disapprovingly*) State pays for it all? The taxpayers.

HANNAH
Would you have me wander the roads?

GEORGE
No… I just…

HANNAH
(*Conciliatorily*) They say *your son* died…

GEORGE
Yes. And I just lost a nephew. Wayne McNulty…

HANNAH
Of course, I heard about that. Gorged by a cow wi' her horn. Uh! Makes you wonder what it's all about. Bein' alive. Why bother? If I was to jump over this railin' now, throw meself down in front of yon container lurry that's comin'…

GEORGE
I wouldn't want you to do that! And Star would miss you…

HANNAH
Star!? Yes! I'd forgotten about the horse! I still get time for a canter round the field now and again. Less than before. Probably better for Star – I used to exercise him too much!

GEORGE
Have you seen *It's A Wonderful Life*, the James Stewart movie?

HANNAH
That oul' black and white thing, where the angel buddy shows him how things are better than if he'd not been in the world, or died young? I liked that film, that and *Pay It Forward*, with that nice Kevin Spacey in it.

GEORGE

I've met him once or twice!

HANNAH

Really?! Next time, get his autograph for me!

GEORGE

Long as you don't throw yourself off any bridges.

HANNAH

Uck, you know I wouldn't do that, I was just talkin' rubbish! I wouldn't really do that. Not like thon vet bae.

GEORGE

Vet?

HANNAH

Aye, yon fella Carmichael. Took an overdose of something. So sad. He was a real dish. We got him out to check over Star when he'd a fever, Christmas before last. Daddy said he was usually glum lookin', but the vet liked workin' wi' the horses. And when he was with Star, pattin' his nose, he seemed *so* happy, he jist came alive.

GEORGE

(*Shocked*) He was the guy helped us with Wayne!

HANNAH

Do you think that's why?

GEORGE
(*Hesitantly at first*) Oh no. Many vets commit suicide. It's a lonely life being a vet. Long hours, lots of stress.

HANNAH
(*Lustily)* Oh, he wouldn't be lonely if I'd half a chance. But, I know – I'm too young. Well, I'd better get Will hame, I've a feeling (*Sniffs*) I've another experience of feelin' something squooshy and nappy changin' ahead of me!

GEORGE
Plenty enough!

HANNAH

All the best for now, Mr Farmer. I'll maybe see you by the river some time, when you're walking the wee dog there. And I'm gonna get a copy of your book of poems an' hae it in the pram, so you kin sign it fer me when I catch up wi' ye!

GEORGE
That's kind of you! Take care, Hannah!

NARRATOR
Isn't that sweet? How it cheers me that others care about me. And so I wander on past fields of cows homewards. By the river I pause on the stone bridge to watch Archie Owen bale hay. No Orangeman he, neither fish nor fowl, Gordon would say, one of the dying breed of dissenters – pigs in the middle – avoiders of extremes. And, if I recall rightly from my last days in Ulster in the late Fifties, a bit of a socialist; a country bumpkin redneck!

The thump of machinery stirs the air, dust particles rise from the swards of dried grass like midges. Archie waves when he comes by on his latest lap of the crop. He'll easily get this field baled before it's time to bring in the cows for milking.

And so I wander homewards, through the serene countryside, along the bye-roads that are barely trodden by anyone anymore, appreciate scenery gazed by virtually only the unflinching, unimpressible sky.

My shortness of breath as I attempt to keep up with lolling-tongued Jess's pace, my perpetual exhaustion, alert me to my general weakening. I guess now I view this world now with a growing detachment. But though these tree- and hedge-lined fields pulsate with nostalgia and current cares, penetrate deep to the core of my being, I've some distance more to trudge before I reach my caravan.

AUGUST

[*Noise of combine harvester and other traffic, as described below.*]

NARRATOR

The roar of the combine announces the approach of harvest. Raymond Thompson, straw-hatted, wisps of grey hair glued to his bald pate with perspiration, is enthroned in the glass cabin like a Western coach driver, hands on the levers as if clutching reins and horsewhip.

Over the hedge winter barley bleaches grey, ripe for the combine's scything blades; oats tinge yellow, second sward silage wafts jade and bottlegreen in swarthy summer heat. Cars queue to pass Raymond's dinosaur on the road, drivers' impatient frowns monitoring rearview mirrors and oncoming traffic plotting their escape.

I turn off the main road, lead Jess on her length of baler twine lead to the brae lane. I pass old Johnny Gourley's cottage. He's sitting outside on an old tram seat, in corduroy trousers and sweat-patched white vest, sipping a glass of beer. Bandage still around his brow; the missis, one of those stout wee bun-tied, grey-haired women with ruddy cheeks, peers out the front door at him, mouths a question. Her recent concern, the break-in when some hood beat Johnny stupid for the sake of a few quid.

I press a couple of fingers to my phlegm-moistened throat gash and rasp an 'hello' to them both as I trot past with the dog. The tart fragrance of flowering bean plants lush on cane tripods itches my nose. Blue pellets dissolve on soil around carrot stalks and lettuce; the occasional bloated, foamy poisoned slug dries in morning sunshine; on several trees green Victoria plums swell, hardened sugar caking like amber where insects or birds have pecked at the most purple fruit.

A few yards more, as I turn the winding corner near the plantation at the low hill's summit, a Buddhist monk resplendent in saffron robes, open-toed Jesus sandals, with shaven head, strides past me. As if dreaming, I turn and watch him head silently towards the main road. As I reach Bethany, I realise our *sadhu* must be heading for the bus stop; perhaps he's been giving a talk on respect for all living things at Bethany, this Christian retreat for juvenile delinquents. For all their success with wayward townee kids, it was one of the headcases from this joint that broke into Johnny's and half-killed him.

And, beside Bethany, the AI station. AI meaning 'artificial insemination', rather than 'artificial intelligence'. I wander in, tying Jess's twine lead to the drainpipe outside, and chat with the manager, Andy Coyle.

ANDY
George! Back again. No Ian with you th'day?

GEORGE
He's doing testing with Gordon.

ANDY

Second stage? The results! Are you avoiding it?

GEORGE

Patsy McFadden's away at the Hibernian parade, I redd up for him. I got a rest, then. Larry Cullen and a crowd are there to help.

ANDY

Aye, I expect a load would help out, after losing Wayne like that. And there's the new lady vet, after young Carmichael OD'd. Morphine, they say…

GEORGE

Is that how?

[*Sound of door opening and closing.*]

PRIMROSE CLABBY

George! Fancy meeting you here. And hello, Andy, how are ye?

ANDY

All the better for seeing you, Primrose. Could I interest you in some pedigree semen today, Mrs Clabby?

PRIMROSE

I'm in desperation for two samples of your finest specimens, Andy!

ANDY

Two? Sounds like it's our lucky day, eh, George?

PRIMROSE

Ah, now, Andy, it depends on the quality of the product you kin offer me.

GEORGE

Randy Andy!

ANDY

Well, Primrose, you know I've some of the finest material in the British Isles, as well as a variety of top notch international stuff.

PRIMROSE

I hear ye've won prizes fer it.

ANDY

Indeed, it has. Many satisfied customers. And unlike my nearest rivals, I provide a home delivery service. My lads and myself 'll bring it to your door and inseminate the females on the place…

GEORGE

Handy Andy! Primrose, you better lock up your daughters!

PRIMROSE

Let's check out your wares first, Andy, before we get carried away with taking you home.

NARRATOR

This office is like an estate or travel agent's, except that the walls display not homes or hotels, but rather the leaflets and brochures in Perspex pockets convey the vital statistics of bulls beneath photographs of each sturdy animal: size, weight, age, with forbears listed almost Biblically. Like a sweetie shop for breeding connoisseurs; see them examining details, countrymen with broken-veined cheeks, in scrubbed wellies and askew flat-caps, tweed jackets or creased overalls, furtive as sexshop clientele, each engrossed in his own private fetish. There are blond charolais, lean-beefed and curly-coated, or sleek, auburn limousin, even leaner but wild as crows, black and white patched Friesians and Holsteins, best for producing cows with milk-straining udders, or the more traditional hardy red-haired Herefords, or examples of the more petite, black Angus variety. (*Mimicking the Liberty X song*) *Sex-y!*

PRIMROSE

Andy, how much is a strow of this charolais wan here?

ANDY

Let's see, Buxford Charlemagne Crompton the Third, sired by Buxford Charlemagne Distelle, out of dam Crompton Suzette Marigold; currently nine years old, hmm, in his prime. Billy Armstrong from up Ballygofey way had some straws of this boyo recently and one of his stirks won Best in its Class at Balmoral Show.

GEORGE

Hence the price.

ANDY

Anything else take your fancy, Mrs Clabby?

PRIMROSE

This one here – Camelot d'Aquaitaine Phillippe Auguste.

ANDY

Mmm, like your continentals, don't you, Primrose? Purebred French stock, that one.

GEORGE

Ladies prefer blonds.

PRIMROSE

I like ‘em lean and tight-muscled, fellas.

GEORGE

You go for looks, not character?

PRIMROSE

Oh, I know these are flighty breeds, hard to handle, temperamental. But I'm after them for their meat, not their minds. For their stud capacity, not docility. They are, after all, males, and just dumb animals.

ANDY

[*As the till rings*] So, Mrs Clabby, do you want to pay me by credit or debit card?

PRIMROSE

Hard cash!

NARRATOR

My cousin Ian wants me to order four straws of Hereford. So I choose a bull from the price range he'd mentioned and organise delivery for later in the week. When I leave the AI station, I pass the Little Angels Nursery on the other side of the road, am dragged by fleeing Jess from the cacophony of barking as we pass by the Cullahill Dog Days Holiday Kennels, then take a shortcut across the Trough Field to Ian's yard.

Jess takes off for her hut, to lie beside the felt-covered wooden box, head in paws, eyebrows twitching as she dozes, while I meet Ian, Gordon, Clint, Larry and a couple of local guys as they whack and barrack the last batch of cows up the crush chute.

CLINT

Ah, George. Can I ask you a favour?

GEORGE

Depends what it is, Clint!

CLINT

Da wants to know, will you gie us a hand in a couple of weeks' time, with liftin' the spuds? Last season, it was April after we got to the last three acres redd up, an' it was so wet they were as black as your boot and we had to plough them in with the landleveller. Lost three grand worth of spuds.

GEORGE

(*Hesitant*) Well, I've a wee trip up the country planned soon, but sure.

NARRATOR

Despite my increasing exhaustion as the weeks passed, they'd just lost Wayne, I couldn't say 'no'. All I wanted to do was walk the dog once a day in silence, then sit in my caravan unbothered by anything for the rest of the day – maybe spend an hour replaying a video of that old black and white '60s TV cops show I starred in. Head too fuzzy to read, or write, or think.

The new ministry vet catches my eye. She is young and slightly built, can't be long out of training. Freckle-faced, hair tied back, looks like some no-nonsense, dedicated farmer's daughter from up the glens. Ian winks at me.

IAN

The cattle've all passed so far, thank God.

VET

Don't speak too soon, Mr McNulty.

IAN

What d'you mean, Mary?

VET

Have a feel of this lady's neck.

NARRATOR

First Ian, then Gordon, then myself rubbed our fingers over the place on the cow's neck where the vet had punched the localised test injections a few days' previously. There were hard lumps under the skin. The young woman held her calliper-like measuring instrument to another cow's test site.

VET

And there's another one here, doubtful…

IAN

Y' can't do this to me!

GORDON

Aw, come on, woman, you must be mistaken…

NARRATOR

Neither Ian nor his brother Gordon's protestations could alter the facts. Larry Cullen was spitting away, out of the corner of his mouth, face blazing with anger as he watched Clint release the cows from the crush and steer them back to their field.

LARRY

Well, George, this is the icing on the cake, huh? They lose Wayne, now Ian'll lose his herd.

GORDON

Ah, don't say that, Larry!

LARRY

I've seen it afore, Gordie. Once they put you down, they keep you down.

CLINT

It's not a government conspiracy, it's just the tests. Sure, it's a reaction to a jeg, but that doesn't mean the beast's *got* the disease does it?

VET

Well, actually…

LARRY

Mary, Ian's dacteured them couple-a cows on purpose, jist so he kin hae the pleasure o' the company agin soon of a purty girl like yoursel'! Don't fall for it, write it up as a pass an' ye won't hae te hae him stalkin' y' again!

VET

Nice try, Larry. But what makes you think I haven't doctored the results so's I can have more of your scintillating company?

[*They all share a laugh.*]

NARRATOR

It did me good to see Ian, Clint and Gordon take such a serious situation with a pinch of salt. For a fleeting moment, we were all at-one, and even potential disaster, the possible loss of Ian's entire herd, was relegated to a lower level of significance, was a mere earthly concern in the grand cosmic scheme of thing. We had each other, were united by a common thread of spirit, and that brief epiphany seemed to make all of present existence tolerable, worthwhile, despite my constant physical discomfort.

Mary, our vet, reached for a plastic bottle of water in the boot of her hatchback. As she tipped the bottle high to quench her thirst, stretching her slender white neck to receive the refreshing liquid, with the other hand she peeled an arm of her now grubby white overalls over a shoulder and began wriggling out of the restricting layer as if a python shedding its skin, revealing a red tartan lumberjack blouse and blue jeans. Her cheeks were flushed red, her uncovering released a vapour of bodyheat and, with it, a wave of perfume enveloped us. A bold wasp settled on the flesh by her mouth as if choosing only she whose lips were cherry-sweet. Jess had re-emerged from slumber, to snatch playfully at a frog on the bank of the sheugh by the mucky gateway to the cows' field.

My tiredness was palpable, the nausea pressing in my gullet, yet I found I couldn't wallow in self-pity when the others were discussing Ian's options about maybe disposing of the herd. And besides, Mary was now washing her hands and tanned arms bare to the elbows with foaming suds and cold water under the tap beside the old byre door, had a smile on her face suggestive of the peace and joy of an angel. The cloud she rode on may have been dark for us, but perhaps it had a silver lining?

SEPTEMBER

[*Sound of an ancient tractor's grumbling engine, revving.*]

NARRATOR

Clint and I perch on the plank ends of the back of a wee sideless flat wooden trailer, our spines uncomfortable against the knobbly shapes of sacks full of potatoes. Ian is atop the unkempt, antique, rusty, cableless tractor. I recall his father driving it during the war years, when we were lads younger than Clint. The bonnet's a rusty shell now, no longer the bright, smooth paint-covered new thing it was then.

CLINT

Y'ont's a *Porsche*, y' know!...

NARRATOR

Clint keeps telling me proudly, as if I didn't already know. We jiggle and bounce over ruts in the moist loam, occasionally getting thrown literally in the air an inch or two, our bottoms slapping down on the hard worn trailer boards with a painful jolt. Clint lifts most of the plastic or hessian sacks of spuds into the house, but I'm not fit for this heavy work. I sit rocking on the potato-kicker, sorting the stones from spuds, pus-soft rotten ones from firm, good spuds – that's enough for me.

CLINT

So, George, Uncle Ian tells me you're heading up country th'marra. A convention? Like wan of these *Star Trek* things! Wow! And you're the guest of honour, a star of thon TV show you were in. There's reruns of it on Sky, I seen you the other Sunday in it. It must be strange to see yourself younger, leaner, no grey hair, all your hopes and dreams still ahead of ye. Captured, immortalised on celluloid. An' Ian's going wi' ye t' Derry?

IAN

I'm going t' Ballymoney mart, no' t' some fool fan club eejitin' about nonsense!

CLINT

Wild altogether! Wish I'd a fan club. I think it's dead cool. Say, George, do any of these honeys that come along throw their knickers on stage at ye?

GEORGE

No! I tell a few behind the scenes anecdotes.

CLINT

All about drug-crazed perties? Like thon *Baywatch* crowd? Is that why you live in a caravan? Does it remind you about the mad orgies in the trailers on the filming lot?

GEORGE

Dream on! Nothing like that. I'll also read a few of my poems, though with my throat this way, I just use a taped version now. Wee buns!

CLINT

Your writin's actually very good, what I've read of it. Other folk have said so, too.

IAN

Whit other folk? (*Sarcastically*) Tom Paulin on *Newsnight Review*, mibbee?

CLINT

Well, I mean, there was an article in the *News Letter*, an' I seen wee Hannah Service down the road wi' the pram the other day and she'd a copy o' it an' was sayin' she was fer getting' George t' autograph it fer her next time she saw him out wi' the daig.

IAN

Less of yer chitterin' lads, there's a yardful a spuds t' surt yit.

NARRATOR

The yard in question is not Ian's homeplace, it's the outfarm at Grangebeg. The McNulty's have a big drier shed here, beside the potato storerooms. The contrast between the sweet, earthy aroma of this root crop in the cool corner piled high with golden glinting tubers and the hops-like, intoxicating heaviness of the drying sacks of barley next door is immense. Ian and Gordon still use this drier, rather than the modern, more efficient though expensive prop-corn additive. Cats abound – over twenty live by hunting, or off the occasional scraps they're thrown, breeding in the shadowy hayshed stacked to the tinroof with bales of sharp-stalked straw. Grangebeg – a throwback to traditional agriculture, a link with the granaries of ancient Mesopotamia and Egypt, of pre-Old Testament times, as much as these Celtic regions.

Ian went with me on my magical mystery tour across the province. We set off early in the morning, getting stuck in traffic jams behind school buses and delivery lorries at Toome now its September and the youngsters are back in uniform.

Ian only has one CD for the player in his 4x4. It's a selection of theme tunes of Western movies he was given for Christmas by Wayne. But there are only two tracks he likes. So Ian replays and replays *The Good, The Bad and the Ugly* as we travel through a brilliant Indian summer day's brightness.

The gardens of Ulster are colourful in their last lush of lawn greenness, with hedges and trees just beginning to turn a myriad hues of red, russet and golden brown, and flowers displaying their final flush of reds, yellows, blues, pinks, oranges and purples.

We glide up the highway of the Glenshane Pass, overtaking juggernauts as the scenery about us extends in its highland barrenness from horizon to horizon a tumble of boulders, clumps of heathers, maze of peaty spring streams. Passing the famous Ponderosa saloon with *The Magnificent Seven* blaring in our ears cheers me, I see from the mirror beside me that my face is as radiant as the autumn sun full on the crest of the whin-undulating ridge.

Shortly, we make a pitstop in Limavady, order tea and a snack in a rough and ready café in that rough and ready country town.

IAN

Y' know, George, it's strange t' think of you as a playboy, as the philandering famous TV actor star in London.

GEORGE

Philandering?! Hmm, guess I can't blame you for saying that.

IAN

Y' know whit I mean. A completely different world, different life, there. Yet you act the yokel here wi' me. Doesn't futtering about on the farm wi' me drive you spare?

GEORGE

No, it's therapeutic. Nostalgic. *You* must be sick now the cattle have been taken.

IAN

It's good to git time to do wee fixin' jobs. Take a scoot up the country like this. Mind you, bein' stuck wi' only the compensation fer the cattle's bad news. I'm not allowed to stock more beasts fer three months, an' the money from the cattle's t' do me t' live on as well as buy in more beasts when the quarantine time's over. Can't even let somebody else rent the land! We got on rightly wi' them spuds yesterday, eh?

GEORGE

Yes. And Gordon's got his barley in.

IAN

(*With a laugh*) Mind that summer' George, we were about fourteen or fifteen, the acres of corn we hutted. Jist us two young bucks! Wi' pitchforks! Horses and kyarts t' draw it in wi' afterwards.

GEORGE

That was the season I ploughed the Hill Field with horses, till the arches of my feet fell. Excruciating pain, but I just had to walk on, behind the plough.

IAN

Aye, George, an' the oul' folk had no time for youngsters' whinging then. Sure, the time we got thon Porsche tractor, I went to check was there water enough in the radiator and didn't know any better and took the cap off when she was hot from the mornin's drivin'. And I got a face full-a scaldin' steam. Me face was cut red-raw. I jist lay on me belly at the edge of the field and scooped wi' m' hands in the sheugh fer some water t' soothe it. When I went int' dinner m' face was as bright as a beetroot. Already blisterin'. And nobody passed remarks on it. Not even our mither! Jist ignored it. I wasn't able t' sleep with the stingin'. Damn all sympathy did I get.

GEORGE

Very different times.

IAN

No wonder you were happy t' head off t' London an' the actin'.

NARRATOR

No wonder indeed. The excitement of the stage; the kudos of working with celebrated artistes, stars of stage and screen. In the early days, Geilgud, Richardson, Olivier. There were heartaches, mistakes, regrets; but I've great times to recall, too.

Our hosts, two tight-cheeked Protestant women, are chittering away to each other in the background in their gutteral, lilting Northern brogues. Neither seems to recognise me and I am grateful for the anonymity.

IAN

The wife and I stapped here in Limavady once a lock-a years ago, George. The last trip she had up the country. On our way back from a weekend in Bundoran. We'd go there when we were young. Always preferred Portrush myself. More homely. Donegal's too bleak and foreign for my liking. The country's more barren, the air choking wi' peatsmoke. Nice smell, but thick on the throat.

NARRATOR

Ian eyes my throat, and the flap of Band Aid over my artificial orifice, with belated consideration. One of our hosts has lit up a cigarette. Its heady aroma tickles my nose and throat, nauseates.

GEORGE

You'd think they'd have more sense than to smoke when there's someone in the place with throat cancer.

IAN

Houl' yer whist, or they'll hear!

NARRATOR

The smoker glances across at us out of the corner of her eye with a disdainful look, but carries on regardless. At least the way things seem to be going now, these smokers' days are numbered.

GEORGE

I don't care. That's one of my pet hates about Northern Ireland: at least in the South they've banned smoking in public places like restaurants. There's nothing worse than a lungful of someone else's pollution. Some of the malls have introduced no smoking, like the Castle Court in Belfast, but sure half the smokers are that ignorant…

IAN

(*Interrupting*) Yer an oul' Victor Meldrew!

GEORGE

That's rich from you!

IAN

An' you're a hypocrite. Weren't you on a pack of Senior Service of Park Drive a day when you were a young lad.

GEORGE

If I could afford it. Anyway, in those days we knew no better. But now I detest it.

IAN

Like the oul' fellas in the oul' days in the parlour wi' their pipesmoke of a Saturday evenin'. The wife wouldn't go near me da's at the weekend 'cause of that! (*Sighs long and deep*) Sometimes I chat away till her, then catch myself on she's not there. Not at the sink; not in her armchair doin' a bit of sewin' or a crossword. You like what you see?

NARRATOR

There's a twinkle in Ian's eye, suddenly, and youthful cheekiness in his voice as he catches *my* eye gazing at chain-smoking girl.

IAN

The oul' daig's still sniffin'? I dunno how you managed it – all that womanisin' when you were younger. One's enough of a handful.

GEORGE

My illness means I've no (*Embarrassed pause*) inclination anymore.

IAN

That's age creepin' up on ye.

GEORGE

Whatever it is, it's a blessing! It's great to be free from desire.

IAN

I niver thought of it that way afore!

NARRATOR

Perhaps I'd great times to recall – enjoyed my self-indulgence at the time. Most of the time. There were times when it failed to sate, or my addictions became unfulfilling. The more a man has the more a man wants. As I stretch my legs across the café's black and white tiled floor, pay the bill at the till, the two waitresses chitter away still, ignore me. Unlike Belfast or London, they don't expect a tip, so I slip all the small change into my pocket.

We reach the outskirts of the Maiden City. Aptly named, for everywhere the pavements abound with pretty young women pushing prams. After so long in the quiet of the country, to be in the teeming, thronging town again, people all eager about their concerns, active, anonymous in their personal pursuits, reenergizes me.

I came back to Northern Ireland, after my rent ran out on the London flat at the end of December, to be cocooned in the womb of home these nine months, glad of the escape from public scrutiny, the pressure of having to perform, to provide and the quickfire pace of city life. I don't want to interrupt this time of convalescence any more, but this trip to Derry, this one last experience of being centre stage, under the spotlight, and of being the subject of an audience's adulation, it's satisfying to be reminded of and to receive that attention once more. Like a fix.

I'd forgotten how good the buzz is. It's all coming back to me now as if I'd never been away from it. Not just polite applause, which is flattering enough, but you can see the sincerity of the emotional affect your performance has on people. And that sense of congregational atonement is such a rush, such a high.

The adrenalin carries me through to our stop at the cattle market on the way home. I'm here for Ian's sake – his reason for venturing away from the farm for so long – to accompany decrepit me wouldn't be excuse enough on it's own. As the auctioneer spiels in the background, Ian inspects pen after tubular-bar railed-pen of creatures skittering with anxiety.

[*Background sound of auctioneer's patter; and of cattle noises.*]

IAN

That's a fine wheen-a bullocks there.

GEORGE

You can't bid for them – your place is quarantined.

IAN

Gordie'll want them. Hughie Maybin could lorry them hame fer us. He always bes at Ballymoney on a Saturday. Hie bae, y' seen Hughie Maybin about?

LOCAL FARMER

Did ye not hear? Hughie's deed.

IAN

Deed? I dinnae believe it. Whit happened him?

LOCAL FARMER

Th'day last week. He was unloadin' a wheen-a beasts and somehow he got trapped under the backdur of the lorry. His head was smashed between the dur and the ground. Some beast must've leapt out and flung th' dur down too quick for him.

IAN

I can't believe it!

GEORGE

Terrible tragedy! And what I can't believe is all the cattle in the country – such numbers here.

IAN

Aye. It takes a lot of fields of stock to produce all those burgers, sausages, pies and fillets folk store in their fridges an' freezers.

GEORGE

And these creatures are all killed.

IAN

Humanely. I heard you goin' on t' Clint while we were at th' spuds about your vegetarian beliefs. Folk need a bit-a beef ta gie them get up and go. No wonder you're sickly, George…

GEORGE

It was smoking, drinking, drugs and fast livin' that caught up with me. Apart from anything else, I've a healthier diet and lifestyle now.

IAN

Whit I don't understand is, if the body's able t' take mate, as well as vegetables, it stands t' reason we should ate mate, eh?

GEORGE

Carnivorous creatures have short intestines; we've got the long intestines of plant-eaters. They're designed for a more fibrous diet – pulses, roots, grains.

IAN

Ah but, these experts say it was eatin' mate made humans evolve bigger brains, *become* human…

GEORGE

That's only a theory. Meat gives us protein, but we can get it from other sources.

NARRATOR

My mind was rioting with retorts, but I was frustrated because my poor throat was unable to cope with the need to respond. I hadn't the ability and Ian hadn't the patience for me to continue. I wanted, but did not get to tell him, how I believe rearing children longer on milk, using cow's milk, and educating them, through passing on wisdom, recording it, in the oral tradition and through writing, that's what helped make us intelligent.

IAN

Anyway, if you didn't ate mate, even if ye breed cattle fer milk, half the calves y' breed would still be male - what would ye do wi' all the bull calves?

GEORGE

Oxen – labour – plough with them…

IAN

Back to fallen arches. Revert back to backbreaking labour! Huh!

GEORGE

Good exercise. People don't get enough, nowadays. With community cooperation, self-sufficiency could work.

IAN

Well, a bit of hard work never done anybody any harm – and it'ud do a lock-a these hooligans th' day good t' expend their excess energy, rather than have them runnin' around in gangs blatterin' th' shite outta oul' folk fer a few shillin', or each other in the streets the way they smash up the place these days..

GEORGE

You see the harm in civil unrest, but not in the wholesale slaughter of other species?

IAN

You wanna destroy an entire economy, ban beef?

GEORGE

I reckon it's going to decline naturally, through supply and demand – or lack of it, as the next couple of decades pass and more and more people change their diet.

NARRATOR

I peeked in to see the sales ring. There were tiers of concrete benches, rows of peaked cap farmers or dealers in overalls and baseball caps, in a semi-circle facing the auctioneer's pulpit, as if ancient Romans come to view a gladiatorial spectacle. The only struggle in the ring was the thrashing of beasts' backsides by the lad with a length of black plastic pipe as he shooed each animal in turn around the viewing ring. Here was capitalism red in tooth and claw; the market place in all its commercial bloodlust. But it doesn't have to be like this.

As Ian drove me back across country towards our rural Antrim home, I pondered literally *where I was at*. I shied away from the reality of death, for all its commonplace featuring in the natural environment – from rotting, blighted potatoes, to seasonal insects drying up on windowsills, to grey-nosed sheepdogs curling up at the back of the hedge to pass on, to stillborn lambs, sick calves, done ewes, road-crossing squashed rabbits, fat heifers going for butchering, to the accidental end of loved ones like Wayne. At least my trip across country had lifted my general moroseness, had restored my faith that beauty, joy, fun and fellow-feeling are possible in this vast varied territory of existence. Little did I know that soon I'd have in store for me a visit that would challenge my beliefs and feelings to breaking point.

OCTOBER

[*Sound of chainsaw working through wood, fades as dialogue begins as below.*]

CLINT
Whao-up there, George! Cuttin' a few blocks for the fire, are ye, George? Gathering in the winter fuel – a stockpile for these coul' evenings. Y'need the fire lit in the grate this weather alright. The nights get dark quick now too, eh? And if it's not rainin' it's dang near it with precipitation in the atmosphere: mizzly. Phew! That wood dust doesn't half get in your throat, an' everything.

GEORGE
Aren't you at college th'day, Clint?

CLINT
I'm takin' a break from the books th'day t' help me da with this injured cow. He put it in Uncle Ian's silo fer t' save it from getting dunted by other beasts.

GEORGE

How did she manage to hurt herself?

CLINT
She jumped the waterhole dam wall. Awkwardly.

GORDON
C'mon, lad, we haven't all day!

CLINT
Da's in a mood. The tractor hydraulics seized on us yesterday. What a palaver, sortin' that out. And there was a badger deukin' about the wee copse at Grangebeg and between you and me, Da shot it and they're protected and thont

buddy Archibald from up the road seen it lyin' before I got over t' lift it wi' th' bucket t' bury it. Of course, Da denied it and they can't prove nowt, but....

GEORGE
Why shoot it?!

CLINT
Those stinkin' oul' badgers spread TB and all sorts.

GEORGE

No proof of that, I read…

CLINT

Aye, so the 'experts' say. Huh! Wait till I tell ye, when Stanley Murdoch went down in the test, there was an oul' dead badger lyin' in his bottom meadow a couple-a weeks afore it. An' there's other stories the same I've heard…

NARRATOR

I follow Clint from the woodshed to the silo pen, where Gordon and Ian are attempting to drive the injured cow onto the steep sloping backdoor of the cattle lorry.

What a pathetic sight she is. Her sides are hollow, the ribcage shows through her hide, her face is narrowed with distress. One front leg is broken beneath the knee, so that she hobbles about on three hooves, holding the injured limb dangling; a mass of congealed blood and fluids mark the sore point, where the white jagged bone juts into view as the useless foot swings beneath her in slow motion.

GORDON
Holy Moses, Ian, she's riddled wi' lice. I thought you'd cleaned up this place? What are y' tryin' t' do t' me? Makin' me take a scrawny oul' thing y' haven't half bothered t' feed. Are y' tryin' t' show me up? Make me look a goon?

IAN
Wouldn't be hard.

GORDON
That's enough of your lip.

GORDON

She's gone down the hill since she's been here at your infested place. I'm not puttin' her in the lorry wi' my quality dames.

CLINT

She can't get up the lorry ramp, anyway.

GORDON
Aye, what are we wastin' our time for on this? Could-a been *at* the factory by now, instead of messin' about here!

IAN
G'wan then, y' oul' ignoramus. I'll take the bleedy thing mesel' an' be done wi' it.

GORDON

Y' kin do what y' like wi' her. She's not worth botherin' about, far as I'm concerned. Put the shotgun to her ear, the oul' carcase isn't worth a frig. Clint, throw up this backdur with me.

IAN

George, get the jeep an' horsebox. We'll get more for her at Ballyards, anyway. An' I'm keepin' anythin' I get, since she was dumped on me.

GORDON

Take what y' can fer her and good luck till ye. I reckon ye'll be payin' them t' get rid-a her fer ye.

IAN

Damn it and I will!

NARRATOR

So Gordon and Clint climbed into the cab of their lorry and drove off. Ian and I are left to negotiate the suffering cow onto Ian's cattle trailer. We drive in virtual silence.

GEORGE
Business as usual? Back to the feuding with Gordon.

IAN
(*Half-amused*) Huh!

[*Noises of the meat factory interior where appropriate during scene below.*]

NARRATOR
The abattoir looks like any other industrial plant from the outside – concrete walls, with a corrugated sheet roof. But a steel chimney expels a steady column of grey smoke that fills the air with a pungent, blubbery stench, like that heavy

pong from Duncrue, that greets you along the M2 or Shore Road, just as you pass the 'Welcome to Belfast' signs. Driving into the yard to turn the trailer near the loading bay, skips nearby are piled high with bones, or assortments of blood-spotted offal that glistens pink, red, white and sickly yellow.

We let down the backdoor of the trailer and the injured cow hops on her three legs into the entrance crush. In a flash she's clamped front and back by bars. A workman in blue overalls, black rubber boots and blue cap holds his stunner to her forehead. The blow of the bolt that cracks into her brain echoes through the high-roofed factory and the cow slumps, shot. Immediately, a chain cranks the body by the hind leg into the air and she dangles there. A tube drains the blood from her jugular.

The clamour from the interior of the factory alerts my attention. Along from our offering to commercial cannibalism, other cattle are hanging upside down, also. But a workman wearing an apron and chainmail glove has stripped them of their hides. Our cow reaches him and he nicks and tears the coat from her back, peeling it until her naked muscle is as bare as her compatriots' – now, no semblance of dignity at all left, she's just a slab of meat on a hook.

Of course, when I was young, we used to see old Tommy Patterson slit the neck of a pig at Christmastime, shave it bare, then butcher it, in those *idyllic* days I spent at McNulty's during my evacuation to rural safety from the Blitz-bombed Belfast of my youth. Not that that stopped me from being a lifelong meateater.

Glib comparisons between this abattoir and a Nazi concentration camp may fall on deaf ears. And those who enjoy their steaks, though they know this part of the process is cruel and ugly, and know they are ignoring this unpleasantness because they don't want to acknowledge it, they'll still affirm their right to their burgers and sausages even if they leave the dirty work to others.

And that *is* their right. Whether it's a moral case based on contemporary enlightened compassion for other creatures or, as in my case, an informed choice inspired by exposure to ancient wisdom, traditional truths, you still have the right to choose to have your pound of flesh and grill it.

But we are still accountable, whether in the eyes of our peers, or the formal authorities, or some possible transcending responsibility. We have the capacity to engage in enough *agri*culture so that we as a species on this planet could produce enough grains, pulses, fruits and vegetables to satisfy all our mouths, fill all the bellies in the world, without resorting to the bestial slaughter of innocents. *If* we put our minds to it.

Then there would be no more places like this, this temple of death. Further along the conveyor belt line in this abattoir, our cow's carcase is slit open and emptied of inner organs; sawn in two, with a flashing serrated silver blade, then the sections are lain on chrome tables as if awaiting autopsy – only to be hacked and teased into portions ready for selling in polystyrene and clingfilm, ready for hygienic display in supermarket freezer units.

IAN
Seen enough, George?

GEORGE
Plenty.

IAN
Th' inspector's just told me the cow's grand. Once the mangy oul' hide was aff her and the damaged leg discarded the mate on her bones was fit for human consumption.
So slap it up Gordon, I'll make a right bit on 'er!

GEORGE
You'll get your thirty pieces of silver alright.

IAN
(*Defiantly*) I will.

GEORGE
Who should I criticise – the suppliers or the consumers? I *understand.* I used to enjoy my meat, too. Now, like most vegetarians, the smell of mince stewing on the hob turns my stomach, the aroma of bacon frying nauseates me, if I eat slices of chicken or lamb my system revolts, can't cope with fats and toxins its unused to. They talk now of creating meat tissue in petrie dishes, but they're missing the point. Even if you don't have to kill an animal, meat's still *unclean.* And it's still gonna clog your arteries with animal fat!

IAN
So, d' you think in a hundred year's time a place like this'll be a thing of the past?

GEORGE
I hope so.

IAN
For all your lecturin' an' harpin' on, you could be right. The twentieth century was all about technological change. Sure, in our time we've gone from ploughing with horses to artificial fertilizers, pesticides, broilers, all this! It wouldn't surprise me if the twenty-first century saw some advance in the ethical aspect of it all.

GEORGE
You think there's a future for compassion in world farming?!

IAN
It'll come. A refinement of methods. All this intensive farming – it's not good. Organics, and ethics, that's where the emphasis 'll be from now on. The way the Yanks want te force GM craps on us, that'll be the crunch. And the Americans seem t' be on the side of commerce as always, not good sense or ethics. They'll gain ground, no doubt; but they won't win through in the end. Because ordinary people right across the world won't stand for any of that grey goo, mumbo-jumbo nonsense. An' all of it's too much fer me t' cope with already!

GEORGE
Thinking of retiring?

IAN
You know farmers never retire, George! I'll die with my wellies on. Sure, what else would I do, sit in the corner and vegetate? There's no craic in that!

GEORGE
Well, I'm exhausted with all this running about the country after cattle. Let's stop at the Coach and Horses on the way home and get a bite of lunch. You with your sirloin and chips, me with my lentil soup. And a pint each and vegetate in the corner there for a while!

IAN
Sound plan, George. Though maybe I'll skip the sirloin – they do a great spinach cannelloni there – a bit lighter for me. An' it'll keep me in wi' you, so's you're not turnin' yer nose up at me plate. But the pint of Smithwicks, now there's something we kin always agree on!

NOVEMBER

[*Sound of whistling at dog; shouts.*]

IAN

Come-by! Jess, come-by! That's m'girl. George, that ewe!

GEORGE

Got her!

IAN

That's 'em in.

[*Clink of gate closing. Swoosh of a sheep being dipped.*]

NARRATOR

An overcast November morning, I'm wrapped up in overcoat, scarf, woolly hat, still I feel the chill in my bones. The sheep are showing signs of scab, so we've brought them off the winter grass to dip them.

The pungent aroma of chemicals in the dipping trough stings nostrils and eyes. Clint's here to help out. As he drops each sheep into the creamy liquid, Ian gives them a dunking with his crook, then they swim forward and scramble out the other end, the dip solution dripping from their wool as they skid back out to their field.

A ewe tries to hop aside to freedom; Clint catches her in mid-air, deftly plops her into the tub. Sheep after sheep passes through the chemicals, only their faces above the surface, until the entire flock is dipped to rid their thick fleeces of parasites.

IAN

Good Jess, here, chew on that.

NARRATOR

Ian throws Jess a bone. Jess has been earning her keep today, circling around the flock, keeping them in check. The natural hunting instinct of wolves domesticated over generations, honed to the perfection of obedience – her master's whistle is her command. An experiment in Russia showed it takes nine generations from a sensible wolf, choosing the most docile offspring each time, to produce the first truly biddable creature, fourteen before a dog-like one emerges. An origin of the species through unnatural selection.

But after the morning's dipping and tea and sarnies in the house, I must face the dreary, nose-dripping day once more. Young Clint's off to his studies, Ian has some messages to do. I've been ploughing at the bottom meadow, for the cod, as Ian wants to put winter barley in there.

[*Sound of tractor starting up; background engine purr as it's driven; later, horses*.]

It's not like it was when I was young – plodding behind a horse, the sound of the buckles and links clanking, the leather harnesses creaking as the shire shifted weight, position. But there's still something satisfying about being in the cab of a tractor, sheltered from spits of rain if not from the cold. Twisted round, eye on the plough behind, mesmerised as the blade runs through grass and clay like a scalpel through tissue; the way the turf turns and falls, brown belly up, burgundy worms scampering for cover as the dirty-white gulls cry beneath the grey clouds, swoop in a line as if synchronised to tear with their beaks. The musty, fresh perfume of loam rises with the steamy heat from the earth's heart.

Jess is lying by the hedge, watching my progress back and forth through droopy eyelids. Her head bolts up; she's on her feet.

A fox darts through a gap beneath wire in the hedge; bounds across my new furrows; deuks between two huge old ash trees and into the copse by the river.

I press down hard on the tractor's clutch with my foot; ease the throttle off with a hand; the exhaust fumes clear; the engine's constant roar diminishes.

Jess's ears prick up. She darts to a whin bush, emits a fearful yelp. A number of dogs are suddenly crashing through the hedge, nose-first, following the fox's lead. I knock the gearstick into neutral and jump from the tractor in time to witness two horses in quick succession clear the hedgeless section, where only a barbed wire fence retains the boundary.

They pull up once in the ploughed field, hooves steadying on uneven ground. The redcoat uniformed riders rein their steeds to the unploughed skirt around the end of the field, direct their horses towards the open gate that leads to the lane. This bloodsport may have been outlawed across the water in England, but yet again Norn Iron lags behind the times. It's near me, so I stride over there, grab the cold, rusty metal and swing the gate towards the post, barring their way with my body. Unaware of the sound of the approaching 4x4.

HUNTSMAN

Out of our way, dammit! You're slowing up the hunt!

GEORGE

You're trespassing.

HUNTSMAN

Well, open that gate and let us be on our way!

GEORGE

Don't order me about. You can't come riding through here, smashing fences.

HUNTSMAN

Then let us go by the lane! What are you, one of these hunt sabs?

NARRATOR

That was when I noticed Ian getting his shotgun from the back of the 4x4 he'd just parked in the lane. He strode by me, cradling the weapon over an arm. The hunt's horn was blowing in the distance – the rest of the riders had gone a different route in pursuit of their quarry.

IAN

What d' ye's think yer at, tearing up our new ploughed ground and rakin' through here wi' dogs an' all?

HUNTSMAN

You think you'd be grateful – after all, we hunt the foxes that kill your sheep.

IAN

I don't recall invitin' you ont' my land. G'wan back the way youse came. Why can't youse play golf like other folk?

NARRATOR

The two horsemen had already turned their mounts and paced round the field to the other side, whence they came. They jumped the fence again, following the direction of their quarry. We saw a figure approaching us on foot, wearing waders. I recognised him as the local bailiff.

IAN

Thon's Paddy O'Rourke, the plant hire firm owner. Bought the oul' landlord's demesne a wheen-a years ago. Now he and his cronies in the hunt start off through his ground, then head along the river usually, rippin' and tearin'. There's three unionist MLAs ride wi' them, and Lord Glencarry from over Ballyronan way. And here comes Jimmy Doody, Glencarry's gamekeeper.

NARRATOR

We marched across the field to the fence the hunters jumped, where we met Jimmy.

JIMMY

Here's a post'll need replaced.

IAN

Aye, Jimmy. Yer boss has been on the rampage again, eh?

JIMMY

Well, what kin ye do? Deng fool carry on. First ride of the season. They canne wait till Boxing Day.

GEORGE

Where did you spring from?

JIMMY

Oh, I was patrolling the river in case of poachers. Heard the ruckus.

IAN

I bet you bag more foxes than thon crowd. Ye see, George, Jimmy does a bit o' night lampin' of the foxes with his nephew.

JIMMY

Aye, we git one or two every night we're out. A good dozen or more a month. That's without bein' steady at it. Them toffs of Cullahill Hunt haven't caught a fox this twenty-three years! All they do's bimble about half-full of port or sherry.

IAN

Well, y' kin tell him from me if any o' them's back near my fields again I'll shoot the horses from beneath them!

GEORGE

Leave the horses alone!

JIMMY

(*Laughing*) Aye, Ian, it's no the horses that's to blame!

IAN

Damn the lot of them!

[*Sound of Ian, Jimmy and George's laughter*.]

DECEMBER

[*Sound of fowl clucking. One shrieks.*]

CLINT
Be still, y' pest! These turkeys don't half twitch. Oh. George? This one's kickin' like a bairn in its mother's belly.

GEORGE
More feathers on you than it!

CLINT
I hope this is the last year Ma bothers with the turkeys. Free range my ass. For all the turn she gets out of them.

GEORGE
And that's with our free labour.

CLINT
Brr! This oul' outhouse is nippy th'day. Less chooks t' keep it warm. How many's that – wan, two, three… seven left to do. There now, that's another one done, afore it cools off and the skin rips as y' pluck.

NARRATOR
Clint ties some twine around the dead bird's scaly yellow feet and hangs it from a beam, in a row with its comrades. They dangle wings outstretched, like inverted, avian messiahs. We're perched on oil drums, newly strangled turkeys heavy on our laps, fingers snatching furiously at the layers of down; feathers carpet the dung of this calf house floor as if our boots were surrounded by drifts of snow. The antiseptic waft of whiskey from my own breath masks the rich pong of turkey

shit.

CLINT
This one's got a quare tough neck t'wring. Nearly pulled the heed clean aff it.

GEORGE
How's your father and mother bearing up now, Clint?

CLINT
Well enough. Ma's been quieter than usual. No presents to buy for Wayne, y'know.

GEORGE
And how are things between your father and Ian? Ian's been quiet about it.

CLINT
(*With a laugh*) They seem to be at truce again! When you think back on it, that barney they had about thon oul' cow was daft, eh? What was it Kavanagh said?: "*I have lived in important places, times/When great events were decided: who owned/That half a rood of rock, a no-man's land/Surrounded by our pitchfork-armed claims.../...Homer's ghost came whispering to my mind/He said: I made the* Iliad *from such/A local row. Gods make their own importance.*"

GEORGE
I'm surprised and impressed. I didn't know you knew such things, Clint.

CLINT
Had to write it out several hundred times in detention at school once – after a spat wi' another country fella. The English teacher had a *penchant* fer ironic choices of lines. Well, there's another turkey stripped to its birthday suit. Damn sure this is the last time I'm doing this!

GEORGE

A bit old-fashioned now, this carry on. Choke me another bird will ya, Clint.

CLINT

Yer an oul' wuss, George.

GEORGE

No. It's the principle of the thing.

CLINT

Being a vegetarian an' all?

GEORGE

I refuse to kill them. Once they're dead, I don't mind helping out your poor mother. Not very good, I suppose. Perhaps I should refuse to help altogether? Ah, it's an imperfect world we live in!

CLINT

Go easy on that hip flask of Bushmills, George! At least until ye finish yer quota of turkeys! Here, here's another wan – get pluckin'! Aye, old-fashioned is right, George. Sure, for goodness sake… houl' still, Tarkan, yer fer the oven and that's it… in a few years' time it'll be very different. I mean, transgenics.

GEORGE

Eh?

CLINT

Y' know, DNA mapping. Gene therapy. All that. Y' know, now, if you've angina, they can inject you with new cells and regrow valves in the heart. Gene therapy. Can *change* things. Reach where medication or operations can't.

GEORGE

Dolly the cloned sheep. God rest her prematurely aged soul. Or body, I should say.

CLINT

Aye. That was the start of it. But not just cloning. Transgenics. They've already cloned cattle – there's this calf in America, Mr Jefferson, the $1 ½ million calf. Dolly was cloned from an adult sheep's cells, but now they'll do it from baby or foetus cells, so your product will last longer. Transgenics means manipulating aspects of creation. Look at the good it'll do.

GEORGE

Good? How's that, Dr Frankenstein?

CLINT

They won't create half-cow, half-sheep creatures or anything silly like that. No unicorns or satyrs. But they'll be able to produce cows that give human milk... Or milk that contains medication to help people overcome certain conditions. They're developing eggs to give diabetic people their insulin shot simply through having breakfast.

GEORGE

I hate eggs. I never eat them. Besides, an egg is an abortion, it contains foetal matter, it contains *bodily* material, I think it's unethical to eat eggs.

CLINT

Then how would you bind flour when bakin' cakes?

GEORGE
Use sour cream instead. Or there are non-animal matter binding agents available. Why, do you *often* bake cakes, Clint?

CLINT
No! I've seen me Ma at it. Cracking an egg or puttin' the white in.

GEORGE
Any negative side effects to this transgenics?

CLINT
Who knows. But it's well-meaning people doing this.

GEORGE
The road to Hell's paved with good intentions. Besides – the almighty dollar matters most to these medicine corporations. Like GM crops – all designed to improve their profits, not necessarily our health or lifestyle or save *us* money.

CLINT
Ah, George! With transgenics they'll be producing pigs that have organs that are compatible with humans, that are human, so they can use them for donations…

GEORGE
There'd be more than enough organs if *people* donated their organs – if there was a law said the hospitals could use the organs unless a person had signed *not* to have this done, for personal or religious reasons.

CLINT
People don't like their dead relatives' organs being whipped out.

GEORGE
But they don't mind if a poor pig is bred to provide you with a kidney, then butchered!

CLINT
They might be able to remove the organ without killing the pig.

GEORGE
(*Getting wound up*) But the pig's going to be slaughtered for meat then, so obviously they'll kill the pig. Innocent creatures shouldn't be used it that way. And they shouldn't be killed simply for their meat, either!

CLINT
Steady on, George.

GEORGE
And I've seen the pictures of mice with ears growing out of their backs.

CLINT
That was just an early experiment.

GEORGE
It'll happen for cosmetics more than medicine: more dosh in it. Nonsense for the rich to make themselves look nice – pandering to the vanity market. And by rich, I mean all of us in the West – as opposed to the Third World where people are *really* poor.

CLINT
Well, I think folk should have the choice of it, if there's medical advances.

GEORGE

And the pigs? Do they have a choice?

CLINT

We give them life; we can take it...

GEORGE

Their piggy-parents give them physical life; and where does the breath of spirit come from? Life comes from life – we aren't little gods, who animate plasticine models.

[*Fade out argument dialogue. Fade in sound of light snowstorm blowing.*]

NARRATOR

The day has arrived.

> "*Neighbours resume their annual cheer*
> *Wishing wi' smiles and spirits high*
> *Glad Christmas and happy year*
> *To every morning passer bye*
> *Milkmaids their Christmas journeys go*
> *Accompanyd wi favoured swain*
> *And children pace the crumping snow*
> *To taste their grannys cake again*".

Snow. Snow is falling gently across the country, though the wind swirls high in the atmosphere. Snow, till trees' branches bend and bare hedges fill out plump as hen's breasts, rooves and roads are edged and the expanses of fields become arctic wastelands.

The countryside is quiet, now. Hush! Hush! Do you hear the breath of silence – no vehicles swooshing along roads. All are in their living rooms, ripping colourful paper from presents, admiring goodies carried from the kitchen.

Jess and I amble past one terrace house in the village where, through the window, I witness three people, hands clasped before their chests, heads bowed, remembering what Christmas is all about before they delve to other special gifts this peaceful day.

Ian has finished the morning chores when I return to the yard. The tracks of the 4x4 show he's driven already to Gordon's, to lunch with his family. I said to Ian and Gordon last night I was still poorly – a recent touch of 'flu, would call in there later, take it easy this morning. So I retire to my caravan, decorated by only a few cards, relight the gas heater, make a cup of tea, with a wee nip in it, to warm my bones.

I doze. Doze long and late. The short day's greyness beneath the falling snow has already turned to darkness when I rise to do the afternoon redding up about the yard.

In the long shed that calf that was poorly last week lies in the corner, flat out on its side. Why hasn't Ian buried him by now? As I approach, I notice the poor creature's chest moving ever so slightly. A faint rasping wheeze emitting from his throat.

The injections Ian was giving him have done him no good. I saw him lying in this very position yesterday morning, when I was scarcely fit to stand on my own wobbling legs, though he was dead then.

I go to the cabinet in Ian's house, return to the shed. Take aim at the calf's head.

[*Sound of a shot echoing.*]

The shotgun's blast reverberates off the concrete floor; there's a twinge in my arm and shoulder; the shot's echoes wrap around me like sulphurous smoke in the quiet, dark evening. Blood spurts weakly from its skull, like water forcing its way from a blocked pipe. I have put the all-but dead calf out of its final misery.

Yet I do not feel content: regret consumes my soul as I tread across the soft manure, regret as I watch the snowflakes drift across the shed's open doorway, regret as I step forward, leaving behind me the rich aroma and irksome scratch of death as life drips from an unfortunate, defiant creature.

[Sound of trickling of blood on floor, and swirling of snow flurry.]

ENVOY

HANNAH SERVICE

George Farmer has passed through the doorway
That leads to the pleasant valley beyond the sky,
Where he now forever roams carefree.
It's left to me, Hannah, to record for posterity
How on his last day he walked Jess by the river,
Tracks in snow show they must've upraised Star,
My horse, likely she took umbrage against the dog,
A scuffle of prints between the hedge and the sheugh…

Jess returned to Ian's backdoor alone, whining;
Soldiers found George, fingers air-grasping,
Frozen solid, downriver where dead lambs often
Catch on the weir, amongst polystyrene cartons.
How do you sum up a stranger, a recluse, a past TV
Hero? All I know is, he meant well, was kind to me.